GRAPHIC LIBRARY™

◆ UNIVERSAL MYTHS ◆

CLEANSING THE WORLD

FLOOD MYTHS AROUND THE WORLD

BY BLAKE HOENA

ILLUSTRATED BY SILVIO dB

CAPSTONE PRESS
a capstone imprint

Graphic Library is published by Capstone Press,
1710 Roe Crest Drive, North Mankato, Minnesota 56003
www.mycapstone.com

Library of Congress Cataloging-in-Publication data is available on the Library of Congress website.
ISBN 978-1-5157-6627-8 (library binding)
ISBN 978-1-5157-6631-5 (paperback)
ISBN 978-1-5157-6635-3 (eBook PDF)

Summary: Learn how a devastating flood swept across the land in seven flood myths from various
mythologies and traditions around the world — all told in gripping graphic novel format.

Editor
Abby Huff

Art Director
Nathan Gassman

Designer
Ted Williams

Media Researcher
Jo Miller

Production Specialist
Kathy McColley

Thanks to our consultant Daniel Peretti, PhD, for lending his expertise and advice.

Design Element: Shutterstock: dalmingo (map),
ilolab, maradon 333, Milos Djapovic, NuConcept Dezine

Printed and bound in the United States of America.
010364F17

TABLE OF CONTENTS

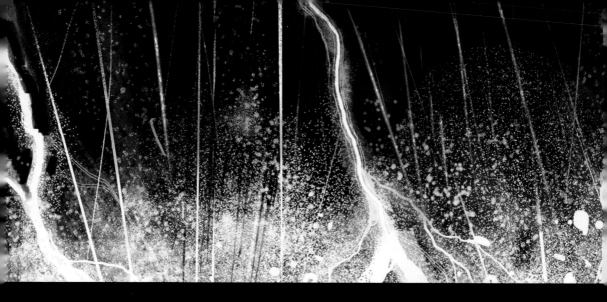

WASHED AWAY

Imagine looking up and seeing black storm clouds stretching to the horizon. The clouds violently churn and expand. The winds whip up, lightning crackles, and thunder booms. Then rain begins to fall, and it does not stop for days. In flood myths around the world, the earth was plunged underwater and life was washed away.

From ancient Sumerians to Native Americans, every culture tells its own myths and legends. These stories grew from a need for ancient peoples to understand the world around them. They did not have the sciences that we have today. So they told stories, or myths, to explain how life began, why lightning flashed and thunder rumbled, and why floods swept over the land.

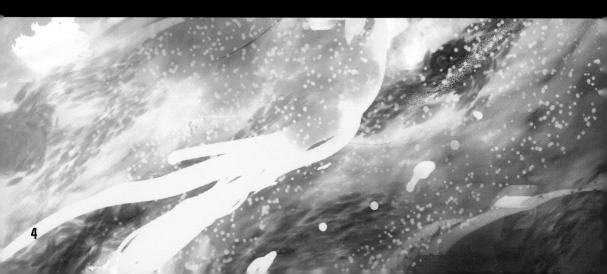

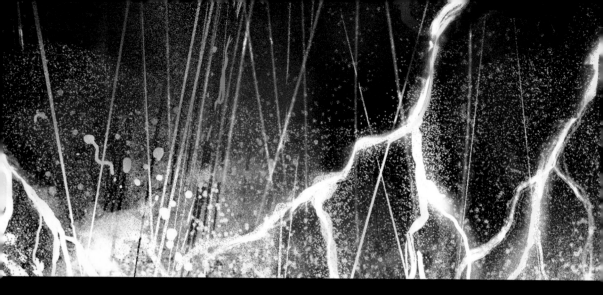

Surprisingly, tales of flooding waters often share similar elements. In the myths, people were seen as imperfect or evil. So a god or gods decide to send a flood to wash away the evils of humankind. But often there is another god that does not want the world destroyed. Usually, it finds a righteous person. The chosen person is instructed on how to survive the coming flood, such as by building a large boat. With the god's help, life does not completely end.

The flood myths that follow were meant to teach ancient people several things. They told of the dangers of displeasing the gods and doing evil deeds. Yet, they were also stories of hope. In these myths, as in real life, after the floodwaters receded, the land was fertile and ready for new life to begin.

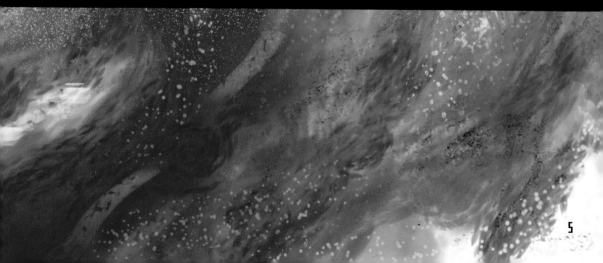

CHAPTER ONE

THE STORY OF UTNAPISHTIM

A BABYLONIAN MYTH

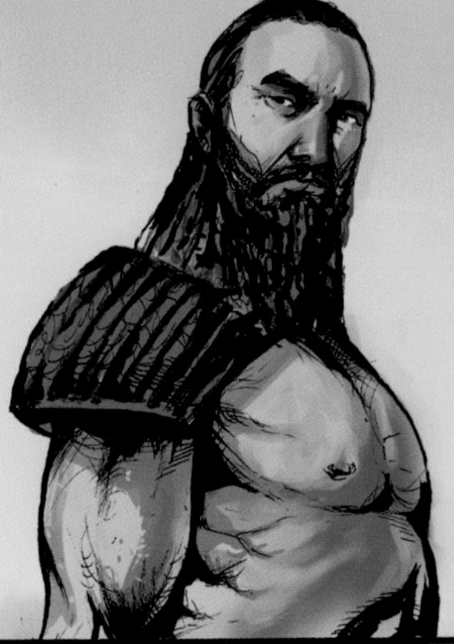

THE BABYLONIANS ROSE TO POWER IN THE MESOPOTAMIA REGION AROUND 2000 BC. MANY BABYLONIAN MYTHS ARE BASED ON SUMERIAN STORIES THAT WERE RECORDED ON STONE TABLETS THOUSANDS OF YEARS EARLIER. MOST OF THESE TABLETS HAVE BEEN DESTROYED OVER TIME, BUT THE MYTHS LIVE ON THROUGH BABYLONIAN RETELLINGS. ONE SUCH STORY INVOLVES GILGAMESH, A LEGENDARY KING WHO RULED THE SUMERIAN CITY OF URUK, AND HOW HE LEARNED OF THE GREAT FLOOD.

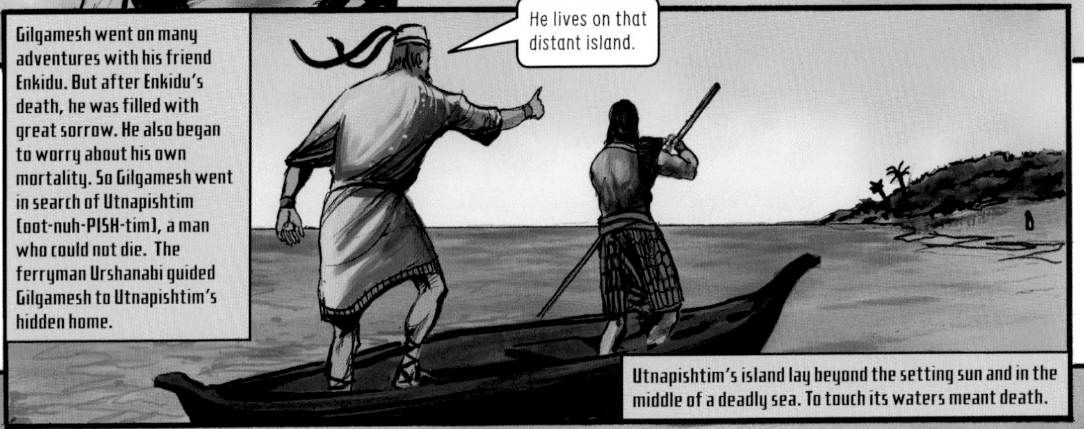
Gilgamesh went on many adventures with his friend Enkidu. But after Enkidu's death, he was filled with great sorrow. He also began to worry about his own mortality. So Gilgamesh went in search of Utnapishtim (oot-nuh-PISH-tim), a man who could not die. The ferryman Urshanabi guided Gilgamesh to Utnapishtim's hidden home.
He lives on that distant island.
Utnapishtim's island lay beyond the setting sun and in the middle of a deadly sea. To touch its waters meant death.

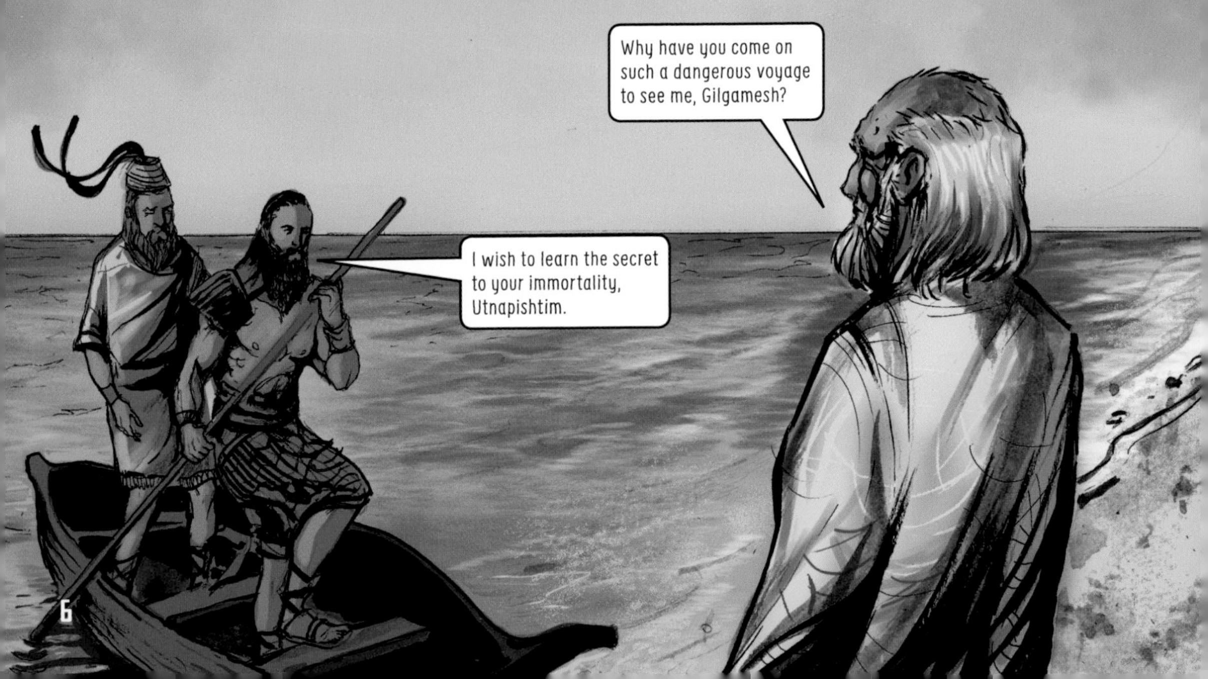
Why have you come on such a dangerous voyage to see me, Gilgamesh?
I wish to learn the secret to your immortality, Utnapishtim.

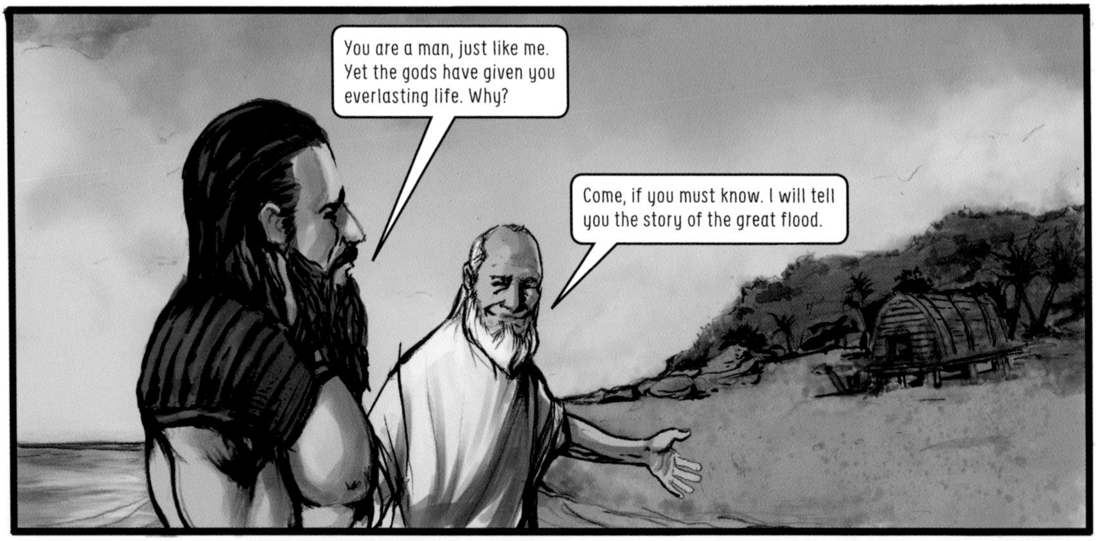
You are a man, just like me. Yet the gods have given you everlasting life. Why?
Come, if you must know. I will tell you the story of the great flood.

DID YOU KNOW?

The Epic of Gilgamesh is the earliest known work of literature. It was carved into stone tablets around 4,000 years ago. The tablets contain Babylonian retellings of Sumerian myths. In their versions, the Babylonians often changed the names of characters. For example, the Sumerian water god Enki is called Ea in Babylonian myths.

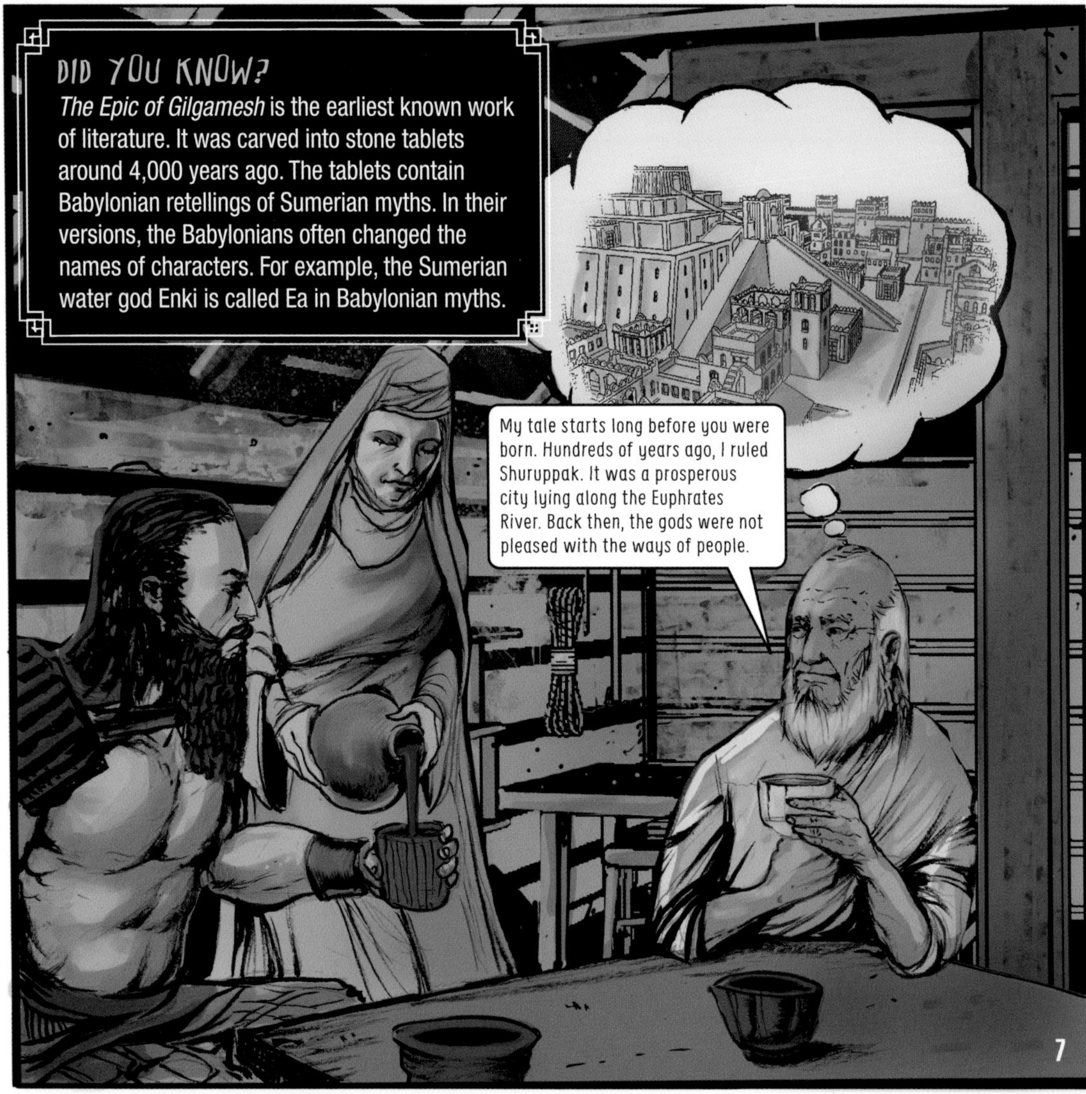
My tale starts long before you were born. Hundreds of years ago, I ruled Shuruppak. It was a prosperous city lying along the Euphrates River. Back then, the gods were not pleased with the ways of people.

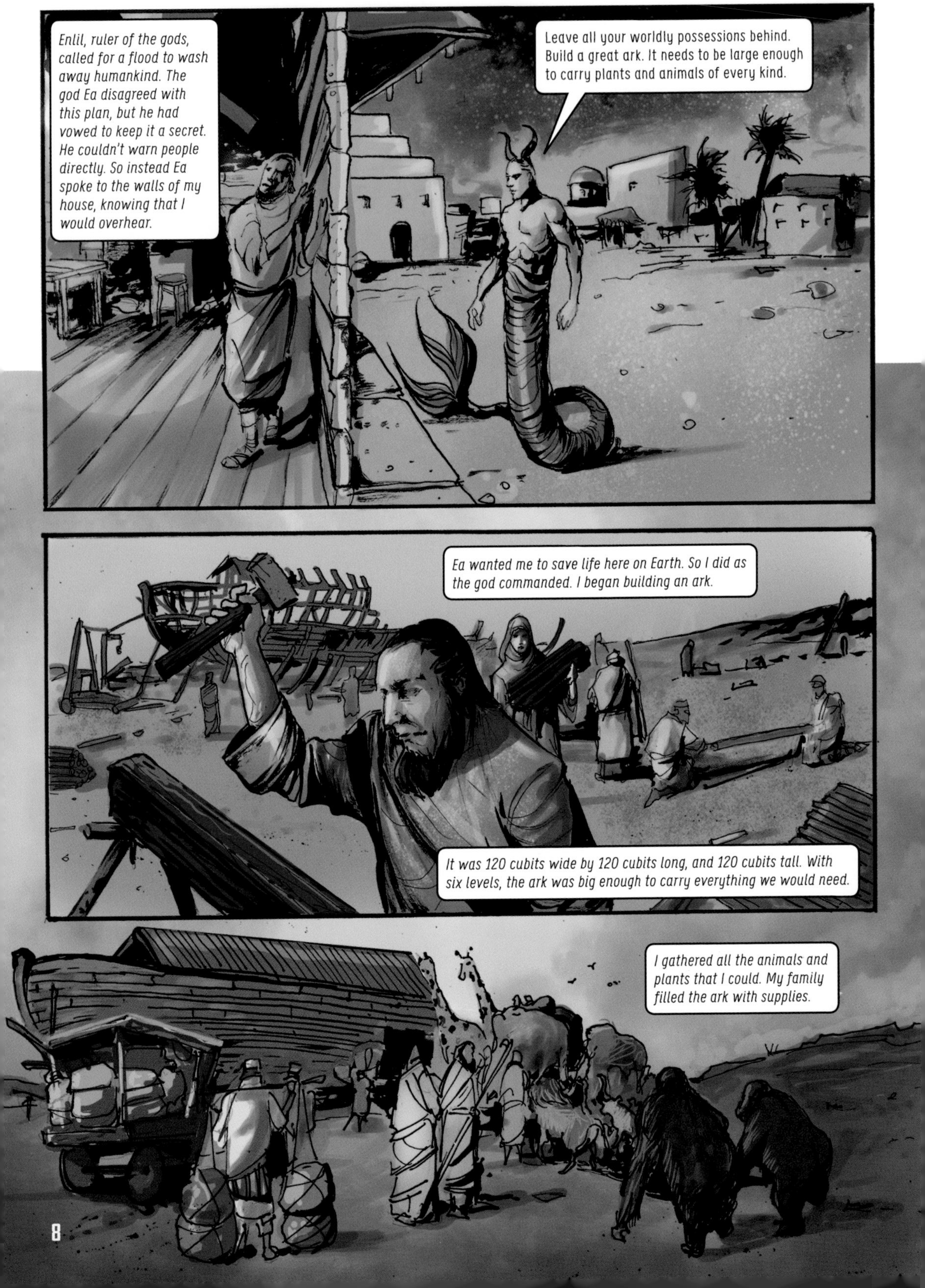
Enlil, ruler of the gods, called for a flood to wash away humankind. The god Ea disagreed with this plan, but he had vowed to keep it a secret. He couldn't warn people directly. So instead Ea spoke to the walls of my house, knowing that I would overhear.
Leave all your worldly possessions behind. Build a great ark. It needs to be large enough to carry plants and animals of every kind.
Ea wanted me to save life here on Earth. So I did as the god commanded. I began building an ark.
It was 120 cubits wide by 120 cubits long, and 120 cubits tall. With six levels, the ark was big enough to carry everything we would need.
I gathered all the animals and plants that I could. My family filled the ark with supplies.

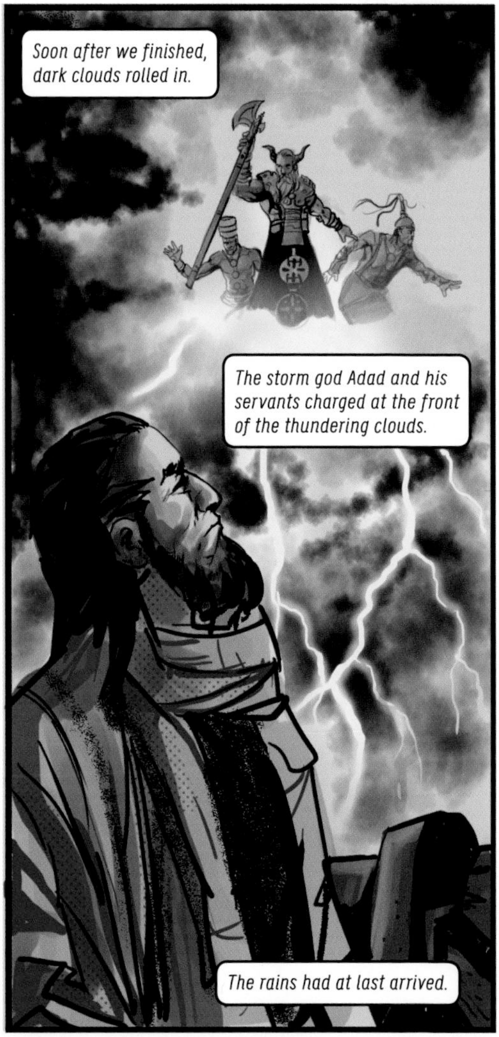
Soon after we finished, dark clouds rolled in.
The storm god Adad and his servants charged at the front of the thundering clouds.
The rains had at last arrived.

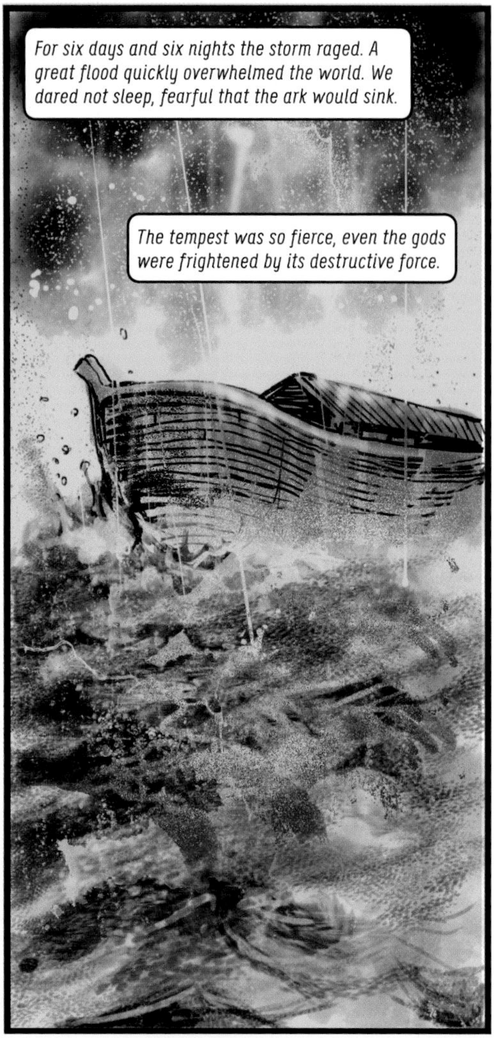
For six days and six nights the storm raged. A great flood quickly overwhelmed the world. We dared not sleep, fearful that the ark would sink.
The tempest was so fierce, even the gods were frightened by its destructive force.

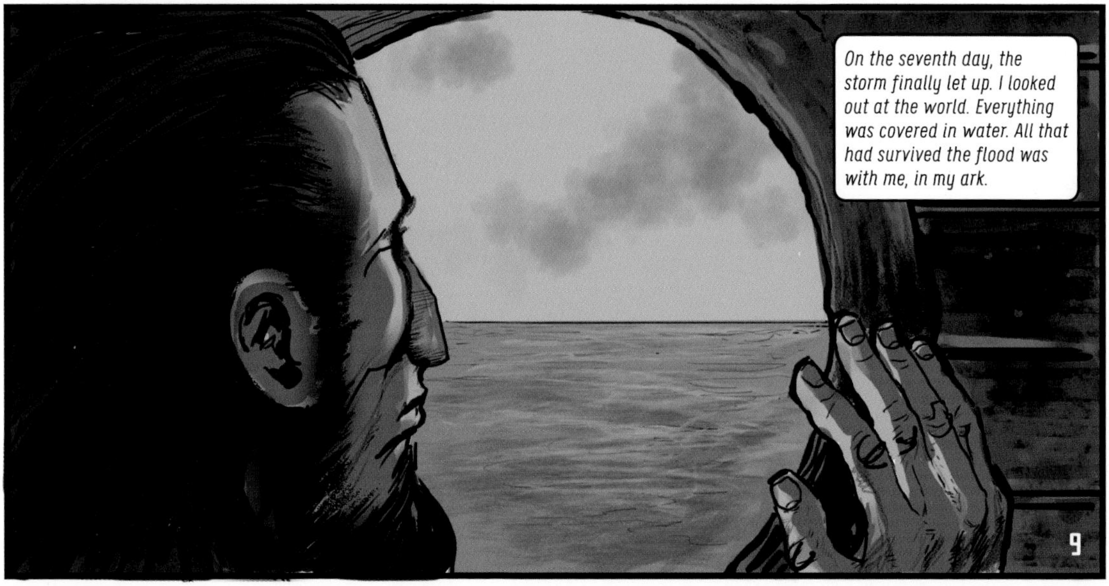
On the seventh day, the storm finally let up. I looked out at the world. Everything was covered in water. All that had survived the flood was with me, in my ark.

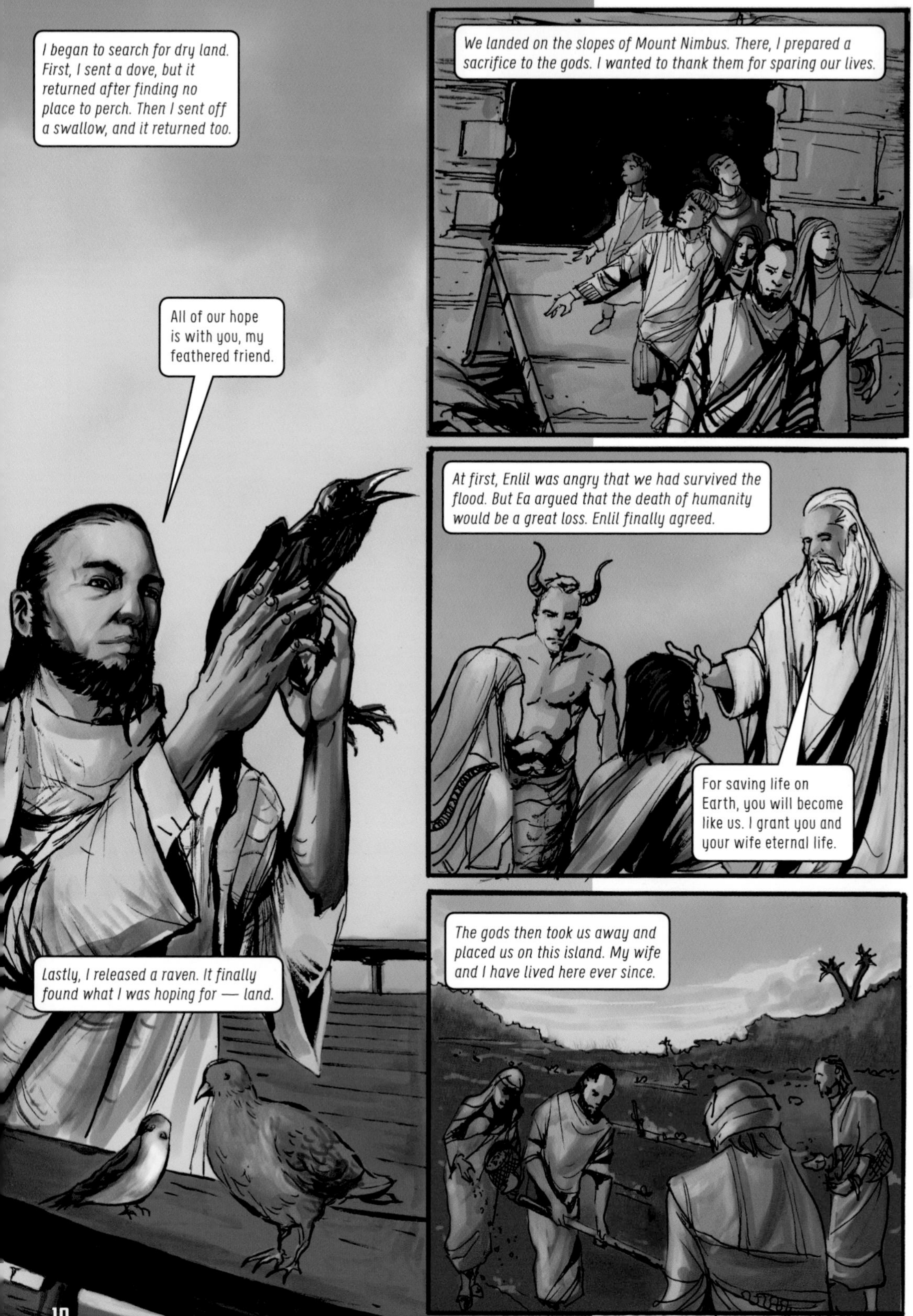
I began to search for dry land. First, I sent a dove, but it returned after finding no place to perch. Then I sent off a swallow, and it returned too.
All of our hope is with you, my feathered friend.
Lastly, I released a raven. It finally found what I was hoping for — land.
We landed on the slopes of Mount Nimbus. There, I prepared a sacrifice to the gods. I wanted to thank them for sparing our lives.
At first, Enlil was angry that we had survived the flood. But Ea argued that the death of humanity would be a great loss. Enlil finally agreed.
For saving life on Earth, you will become like us. I grant you and your wife eternal life.
The gods then took us away and placed us on this island. My wife and I have lived here ever since.

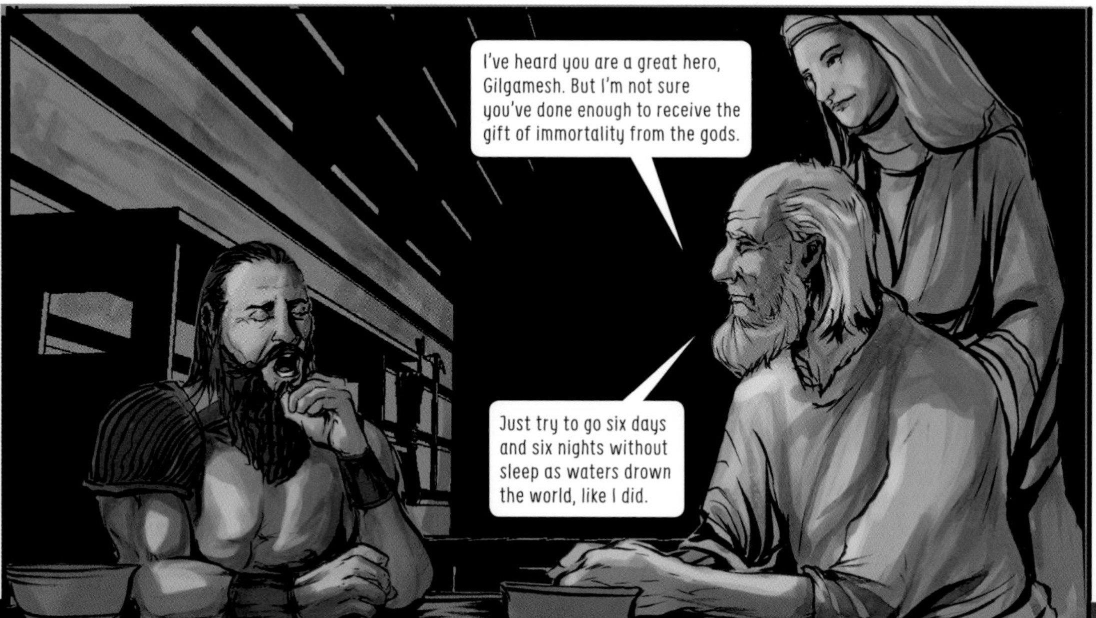
I've heard you are a great hero, Gilgamesh. But I'm not sure you've done enough to receive the gift of immortality from the gods.
Just try to go six days and six nights without sleep as waters drown the world, like I did.

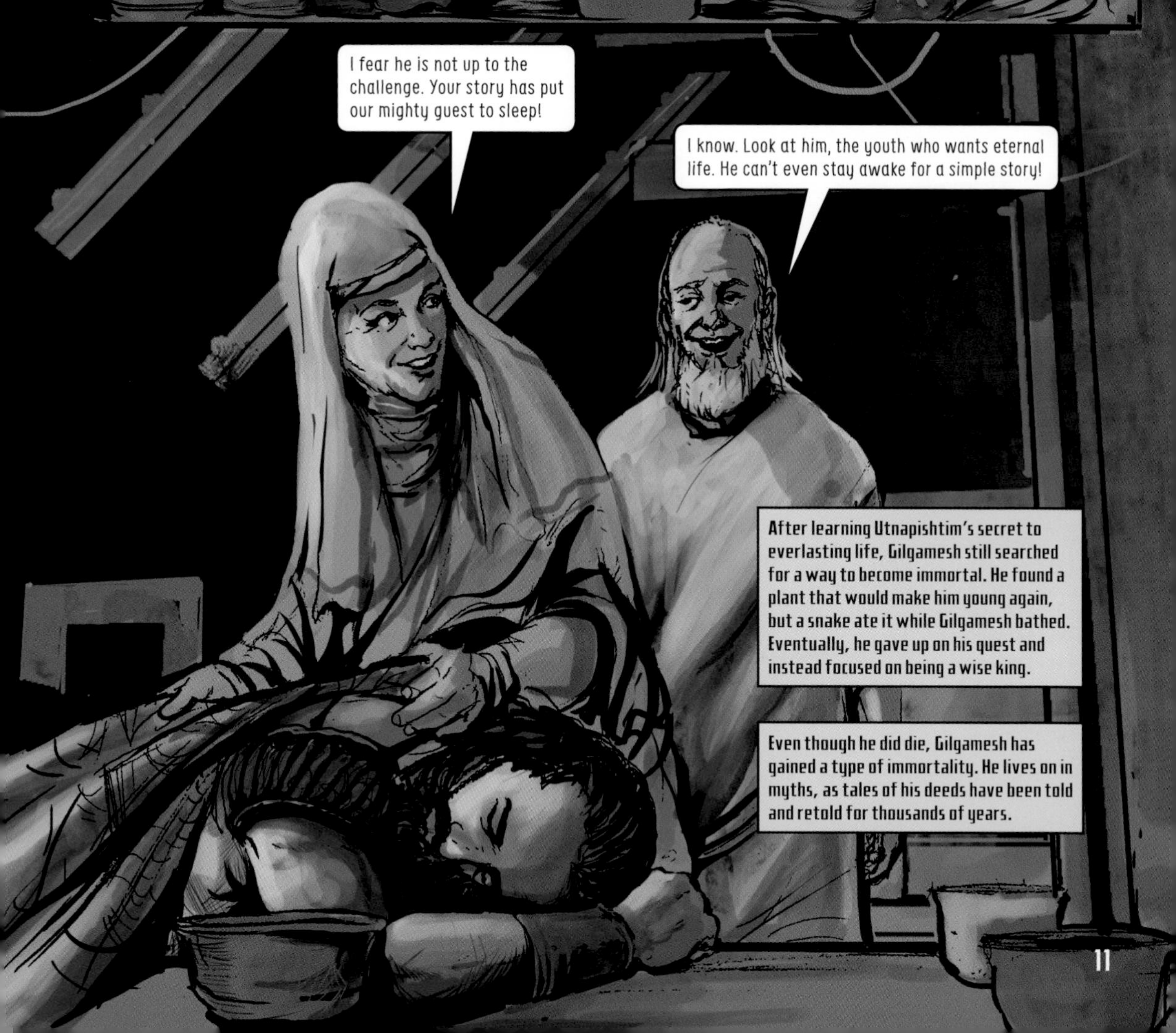
I fear he is not up to the challenge. Your story has put our mighty guest to sleep!
I know. Look at him, the youth who wants eternal life. He can't even stay awake for a simple story!
After learning Utnapishtim's secret to everlasting life, Gilgamesh still searched for a way to become immortal. He found a plant that would make him young again, but a snake ate it while Gilgamesh bathed. Eventually, he gave up on his quest and instead focused on being a wise king.
Even though he did die, Gilgamesh has gained a type of immortality. He lives on in myths, as tales of his deeds have been told and retold for thousands of years.

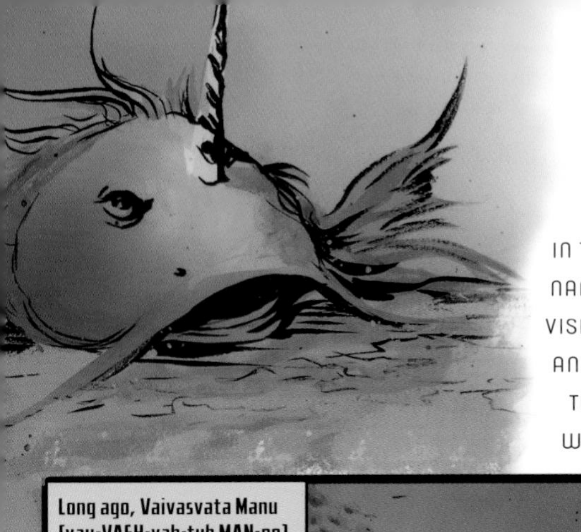

CHAPTER TWO

MANU AND THE FISH

AN INDIAN MYTH

IN THE FOLKLORE OF INDIA, THERE ARE THREE MAIN GODS. THEIR NAMES ARE BRAHAM THE CREATOR, SHIVA THE DESTROYER, AND VISHNU (**VISH**-NOO) THE PRESERVER. VISHNU PROTECTS CREATION AND MAINTAINS THE BALANCE OF GOOD AND EVIL. IN THIS MYTH, THE GOD CHANGED INTO A FISH AND SEARCHED FOR SOMEONE WORTHY TO WARN OF A GREAT DANGER — THE COMING FLOOD.

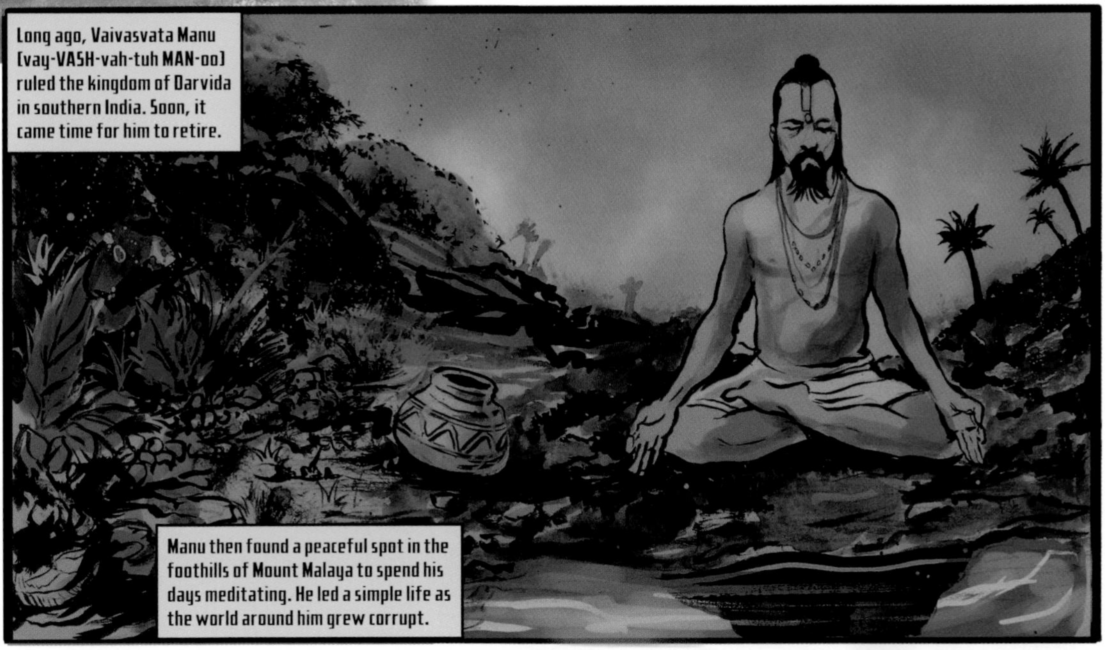
Long ago, Vaivasvata Manu (vay-VASH-vah-tuh MAN-oo) ruled the kingdom of Darvida in southern India. Soon, it came time for him to retire.
Manu then found a peaceful spot in the foothills of Mount Malaya to spend his days meditating. He led a simple life as the world around him grew corrupt.

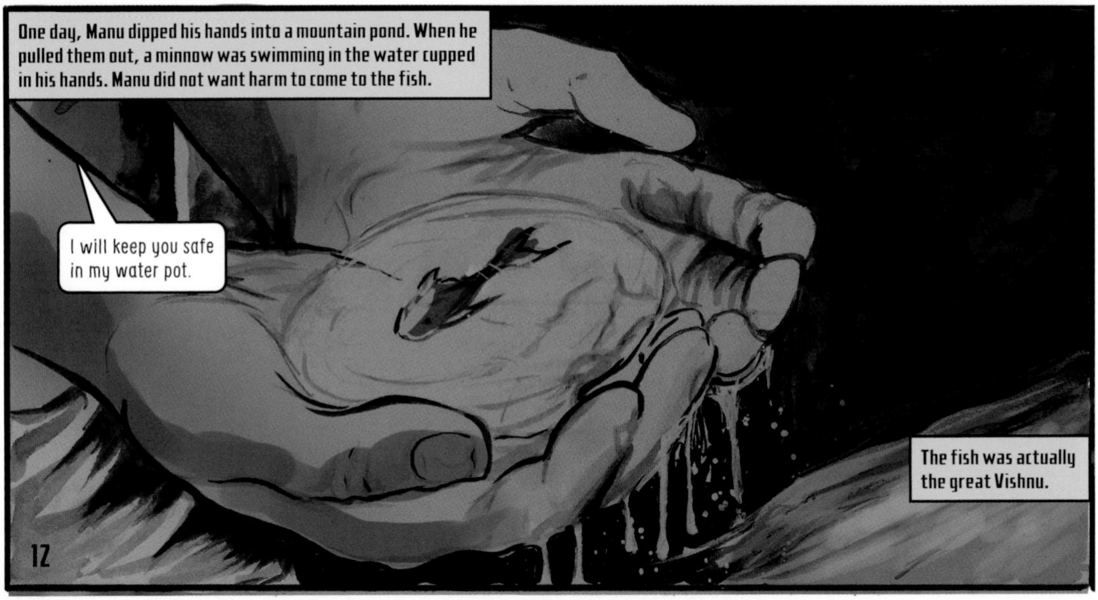
One day, Manu dipped his hands into a mountain pond. When he pulled them out, a minnow was swimming in the water cupped in his hands. Manu did not want harm to come to the fish.
I will keep you safe in my water pot.
The fish was actually the great Vishnu.

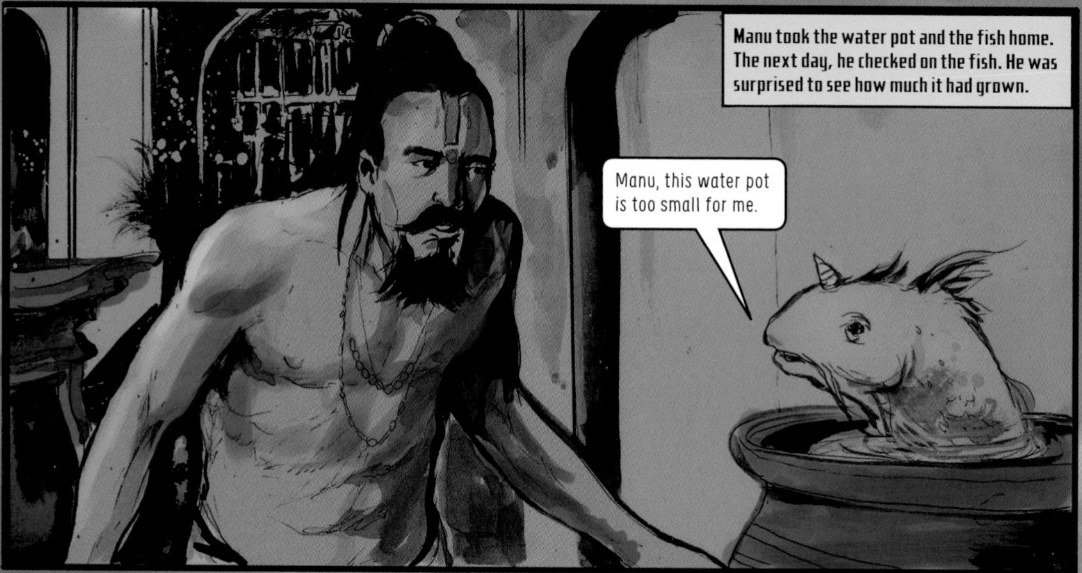
Manu took the water pot and the fish home. The next day, he checked on the fish. He was surprised to see how much it had grown.
Manu, this water pot is too small for me.

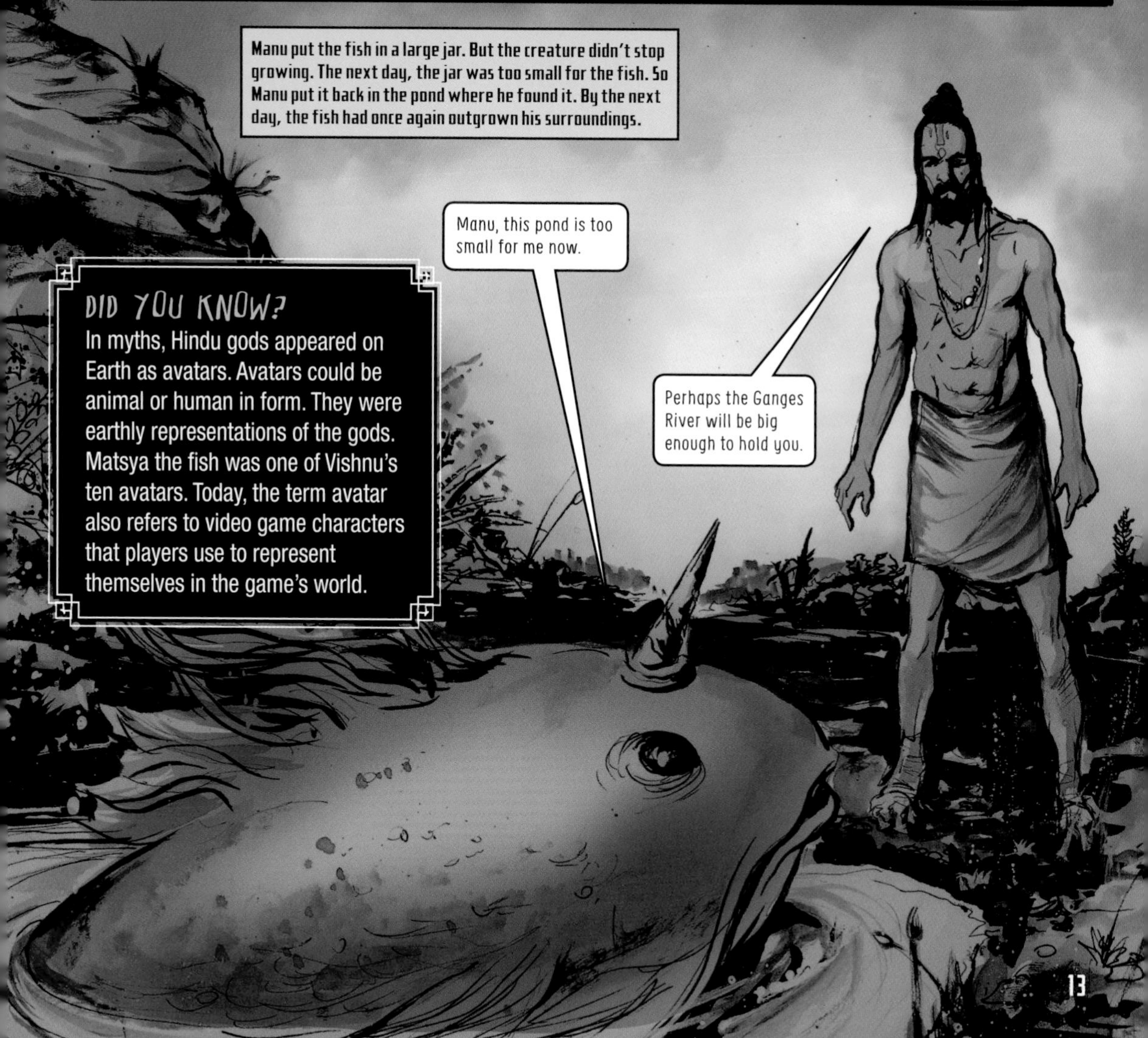
Manu put the fish in a large jar. But the creature didn't stop growing. The next day, the jar was too small for the fish. So Manu put it back in the pond where he found it. By the next day, the fish had once again outgrown his surroundings.
Manu, this pond is too small for me now.
Perhaps the Ganges River will be big enough to hold you.

DID YOU KNOW?

In myths, Hindu gods appeared on Earth as avatars. Avatars could be animal or human in form. They were earthly representations of the gods. Matsya the fish was one of Vishnu's ten avatars. Today, the term avatar also refers to video game characters that players use to represent themselves in the game's world.

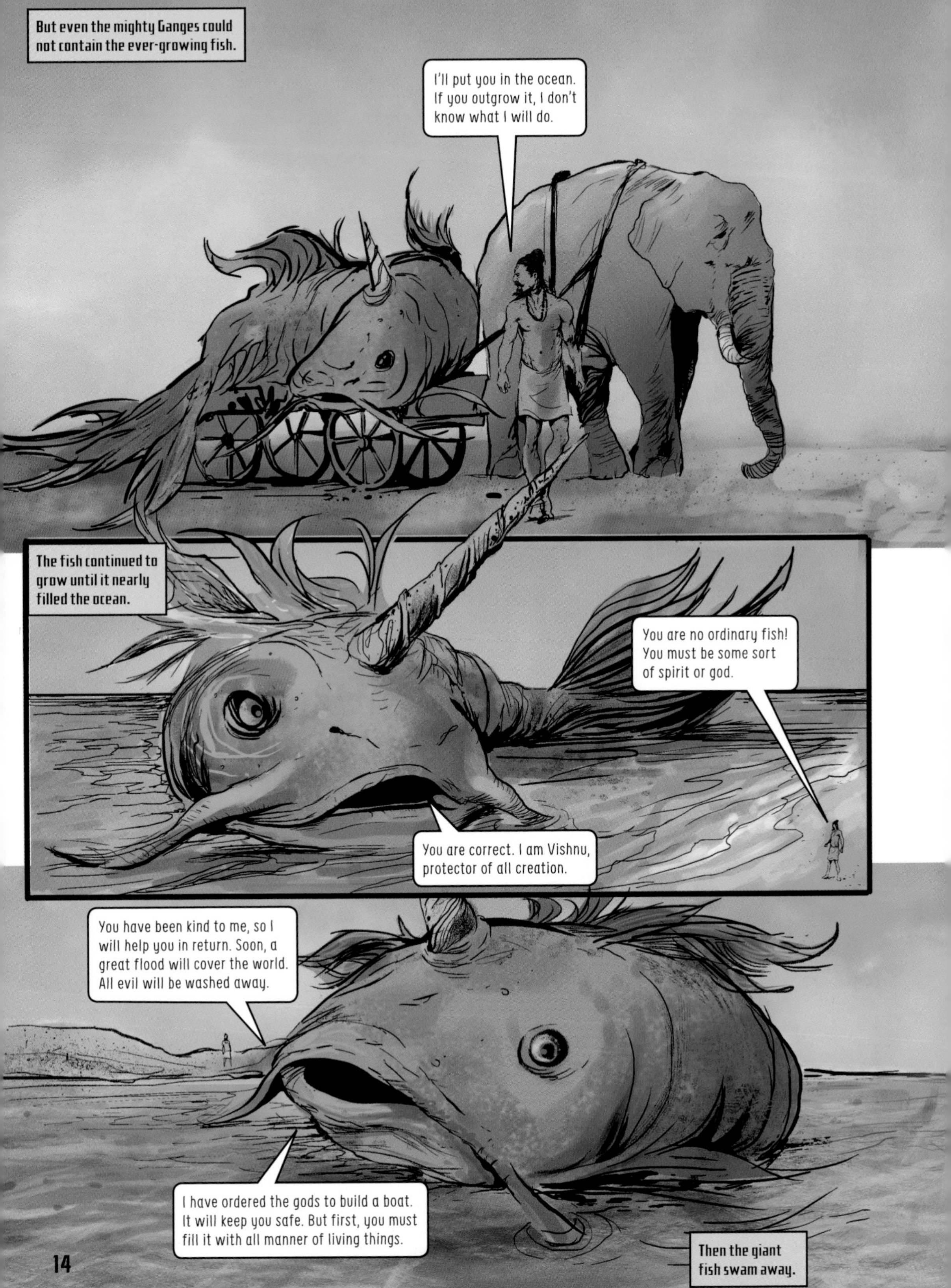

But even the mighty Ganges could not contain the ever-growing fish.
I'll put you in the ocean. If you outgrow it, I don't know what I will do.
The fish continued to grow until it nearly filled the ocean.
You are no ordinary fish! You must be some sort of spirit or god.
You are correct. I am Vishnu, protector of all creation.
You have been kind to me, so I will help you in return. Soon, a great flood will cover the world. All evil will be washed away.
I have ordered the gods to build a boat. It will keep you safe. But first, you must fill it with all manner of living things.
Then the giant fish swam away.

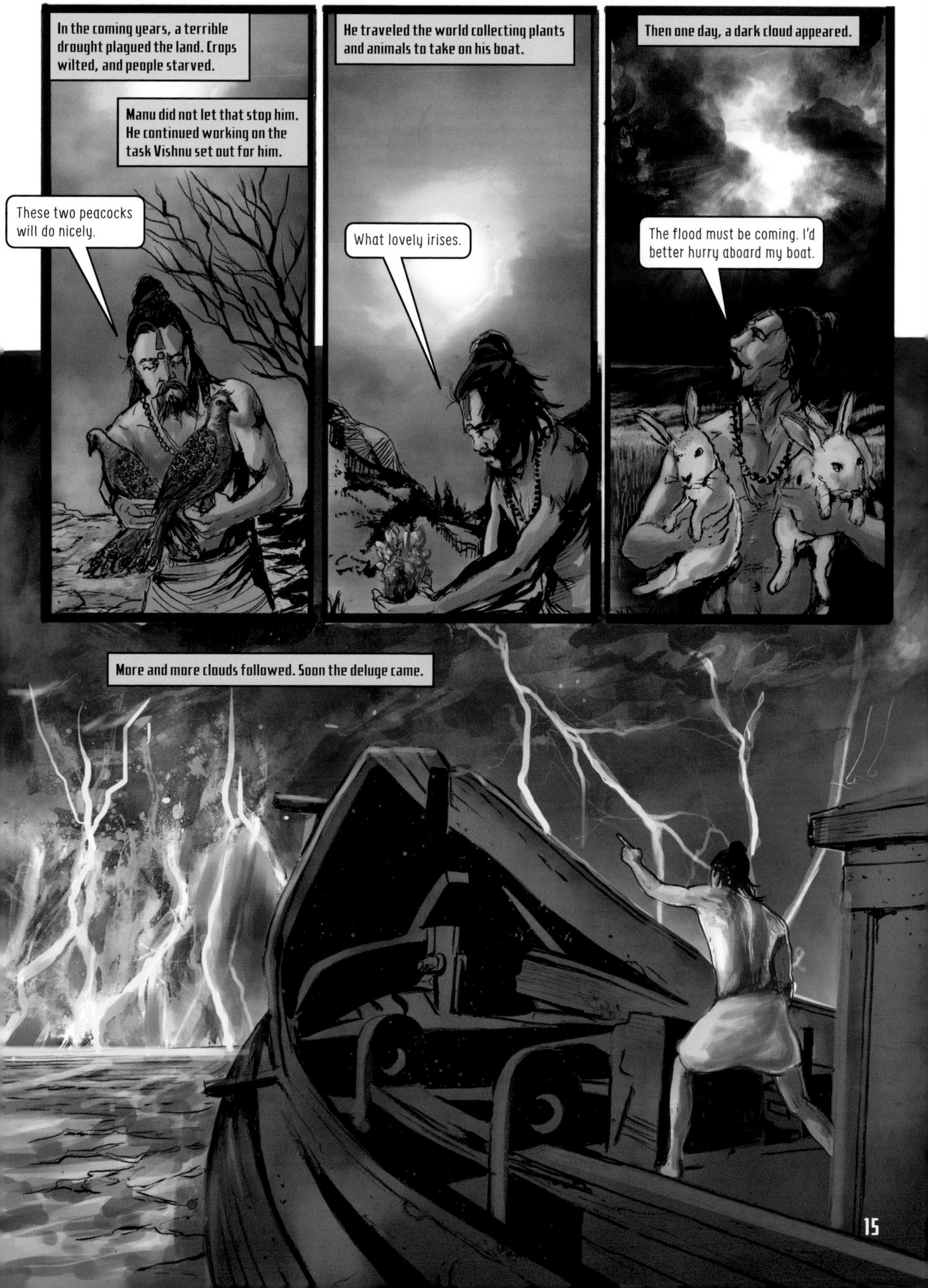
In the coming years, a terrible drought plagued the land. Crops wilted, and people starved.
Manu did not let that stop him. He continued working on the task Vishnu set out for him.
These two peacocks will do nicely.
He traveled the world collecting plants and animals to take on his boat.
What lovely irises.
Then one day, a dark cloud appeared.
The flood must be coming. I'd better hurry aboard my boat.
More and more clouds followed. Soon the deluge came.

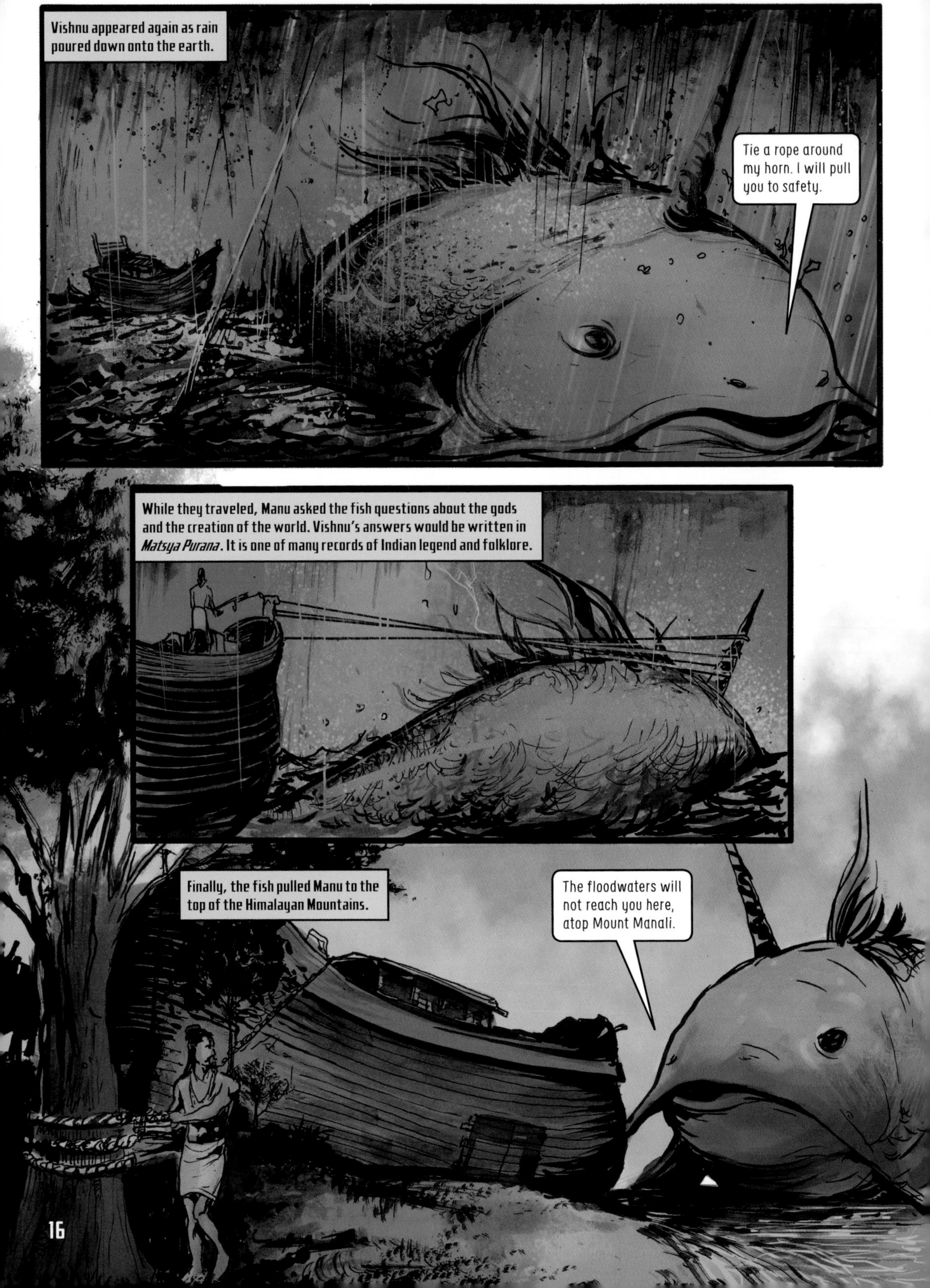

Vishnu appeared again as rain poured down onto the earth.
Tie a rope around my horn. I will pull you to safety.
While they traveled, Manu asked the fish questions about the gods and the creation of the world. Vishnu's answers would be written in *Matsya Purana*. It is one of many records of Indian legend and folklore.
Finally, the fish pulled Manu to the top of the Himalayan Mountains.
The floodwaters will not reach you here, atop Mount Manali.

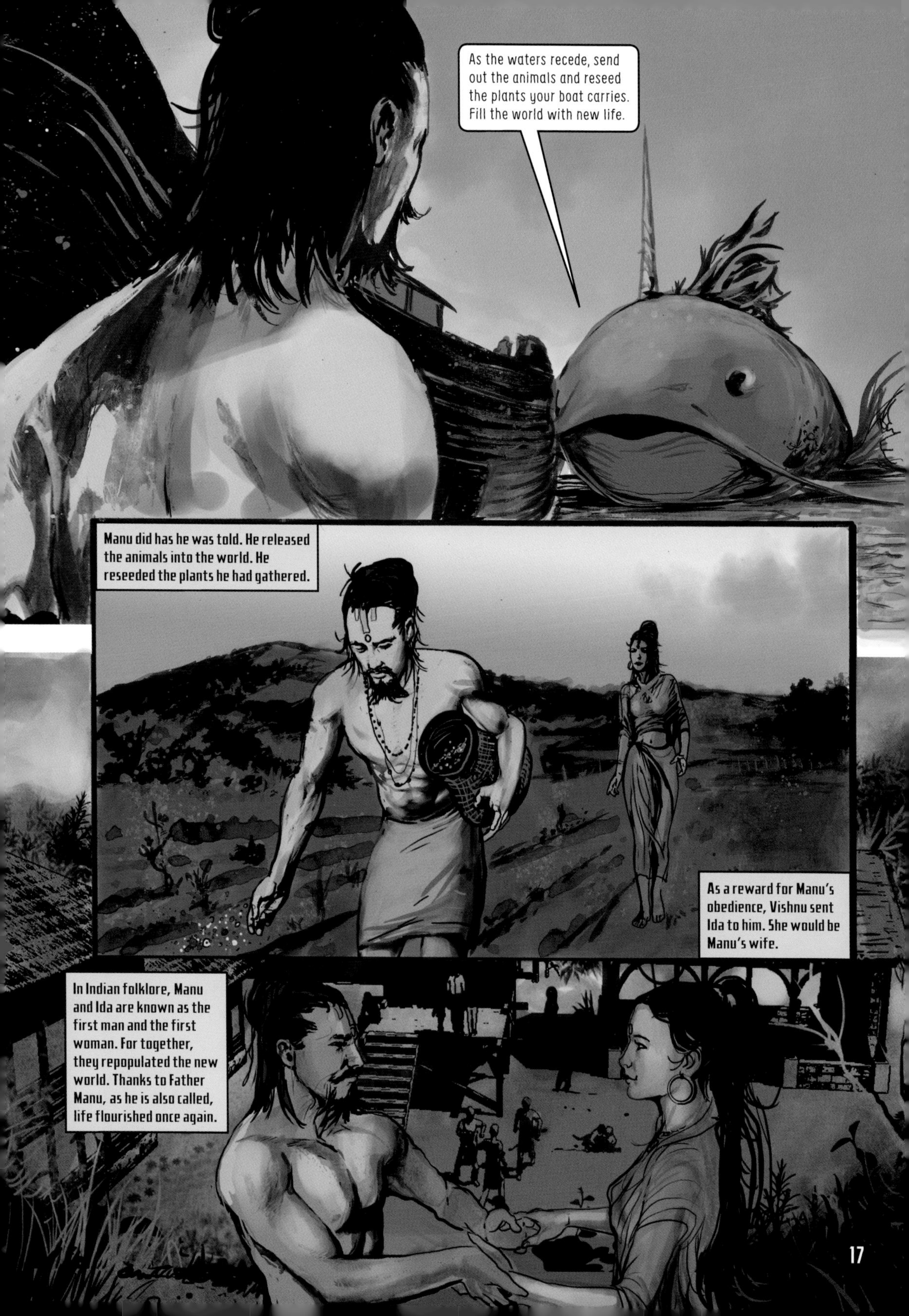
As the waters recede, send out the animals and reseed the plants your boat carries. Fill the world with new life.
Manu did has he was told. He released the animals into the world. He reseeded the plants he had gathered.
As a reward for Manu's obedience, Vishnu sent Ida to him. She would be Manu's wife.
In Indian folklore, Manu and Ida are known as the first man and the first woman. For together, they repopulated the new world. Thanks to Father Manu, as he is also called, life flourished once again.

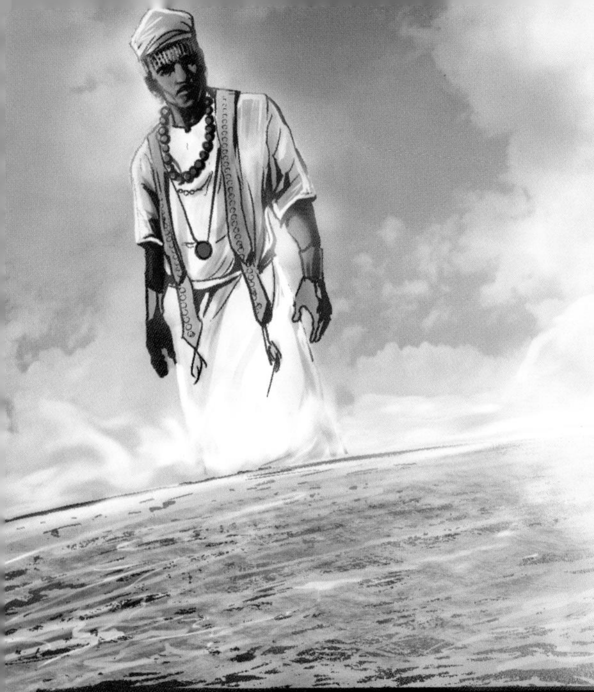

CHAPTER THREE

THE CITY OF ILE-IFE

A YORUBA MYTH

IN THE YORUBA MYTHS FROM WEST AFRICA, ALL THAT EXISTED AT FIRST WERE THE SKY ABOVE AND THE WATER BELOW. THE GOD OLORUN RULED THE SKY, AND THE GODDESS OLOKUN RULED WHAT WAS BELOW. AMONG OLORUN'S CHILDREN WERE ORUNMILA AND OBATALA. TOGETHER, THE TWO BROTHERS PLAYED AN IMPORTANT PART IN THIS TALE OF THE WORLD'S CREATION AND THE TERRIBLE FLOOD THAT FOLLOWED.

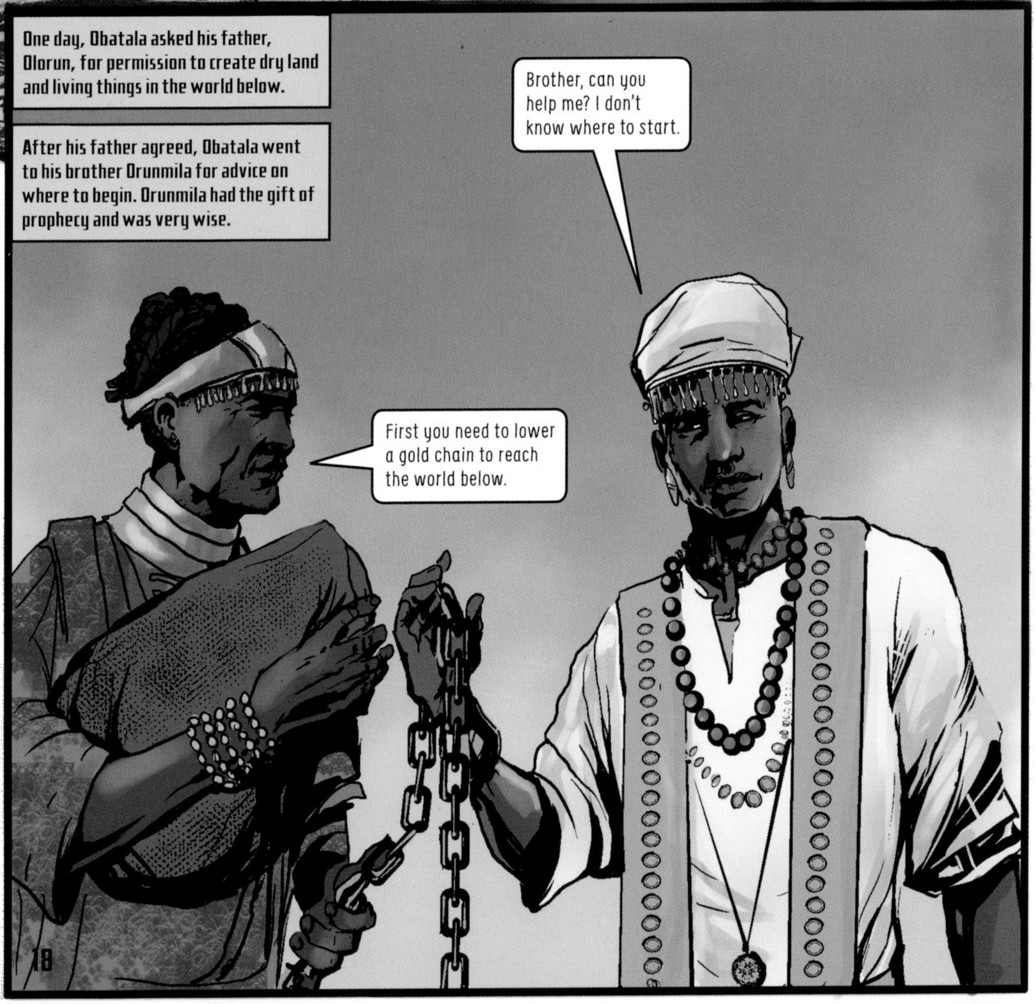
One day, Obatala asked his father, Olorun, for permission to create dry land and living things in the world below.
After his father agreed, Obatala went to his brother Orunmila for advice on where to begin. Orunmila had the gift of prophecy and was very wise.
Brother, can you help me? I don't know where to start.
First you need to lower a gold chain to reach the world below.

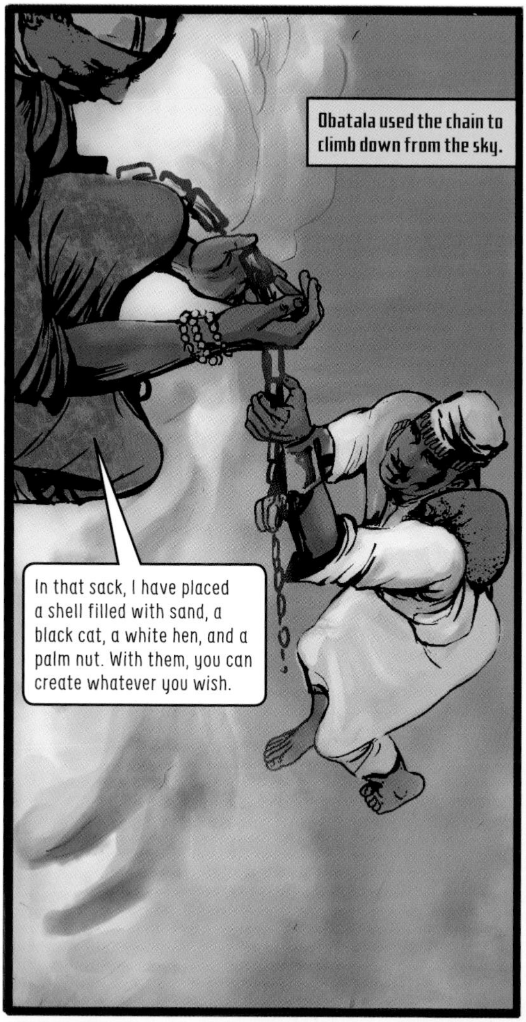
Obatala used the chain to climb down from the sky.
In that sack, I have placed a shell filled with sand, a black cat, a white hen, and a palm nut. With them, you can create whatever you wish.

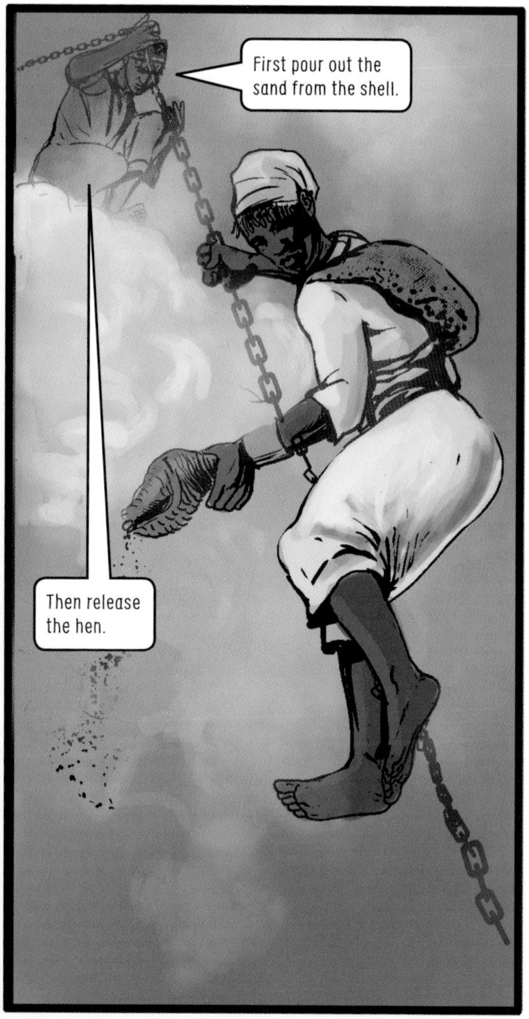
First pour out the sand from the shell.
Then release the hen.

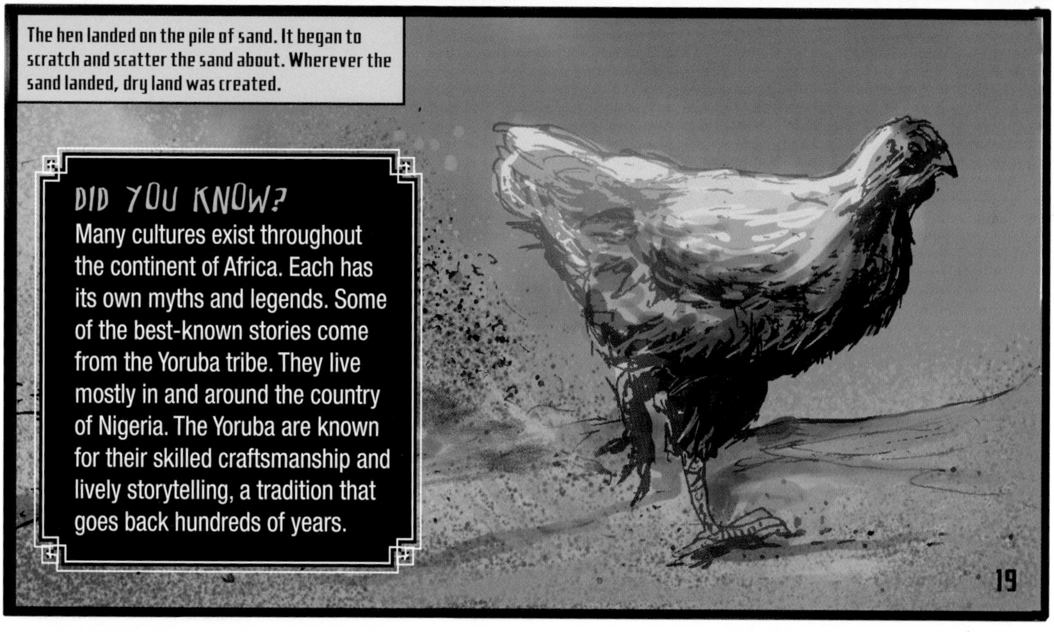
The hen landed on the pile of sand. It began to scratch and scatter the sand about. Wherever the sand landed, dry land was created.

DID YOU KNOW?

Many cultures exist throughout the continent of Africa. Each has its own myths and legends. Some of the best-known stories come from the Yoruba tribe. They live mostly in and around the country of Nigeria. The Yoruba are known for their skilled craftsmanship and lively storytelling, a tradition that goes back hundreds of years.

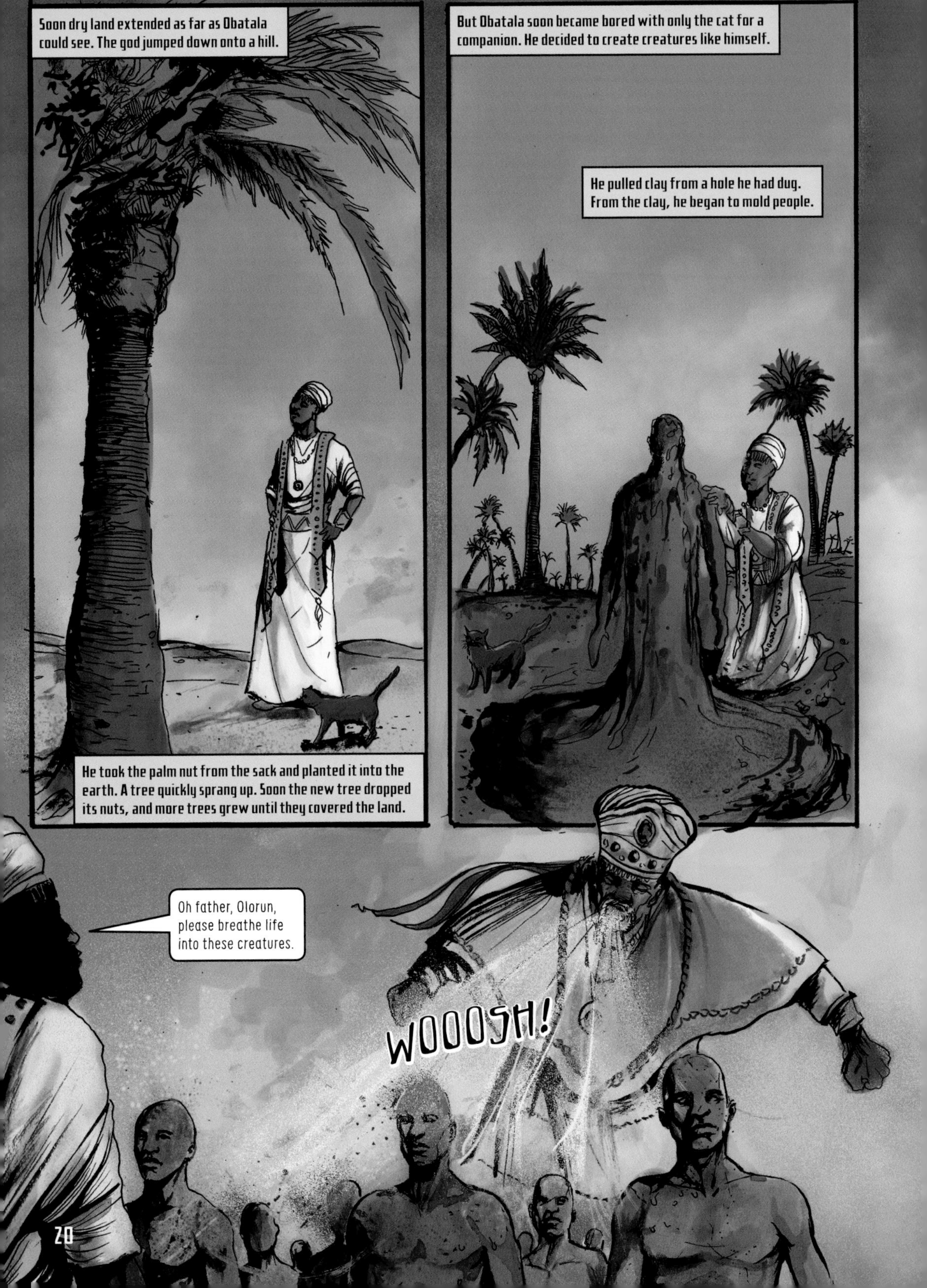
Soon dry land extended as far as Obatala could see. The god jumped down onto a hill.
He took the palm nut from the sack and planted it into the earth. A tree quickly sprang up. Soon the new tree dropped its nuts, and more trees grew until they covered the land.
But Obatala soon became bored with only the cat for a companion. He decided to create creatures like himself.
He pulled clay from a hole he had dug. From the clay, he began to mold people.
Oh father, Olorun, please breathe life into these creatures.
WOOOSH!

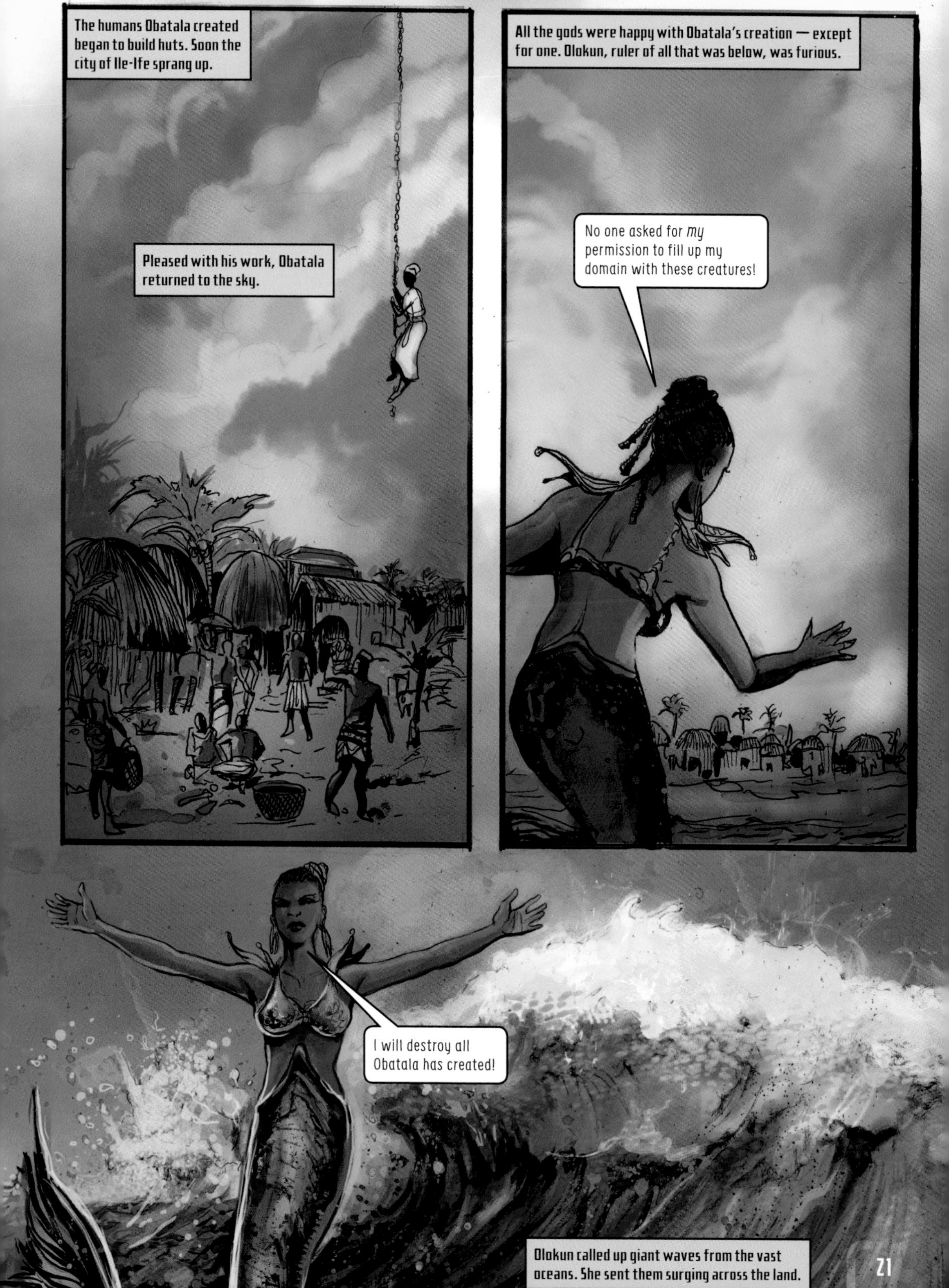

The humans Obatala created began to build huts. Soon the city of Ile-Ife sprang up.
Pleased with his work, Obatala returned to the sky.
All the gods were happy with Obatala's creation — except for one. Olokun, ruler of all that was below, was furious.
No one asked for *my* permission to fill up my domain with these creatures!
I will destroy all Obatala has created!
Olokun called up giant waves from the vast oceans. She sent them surging across the land.

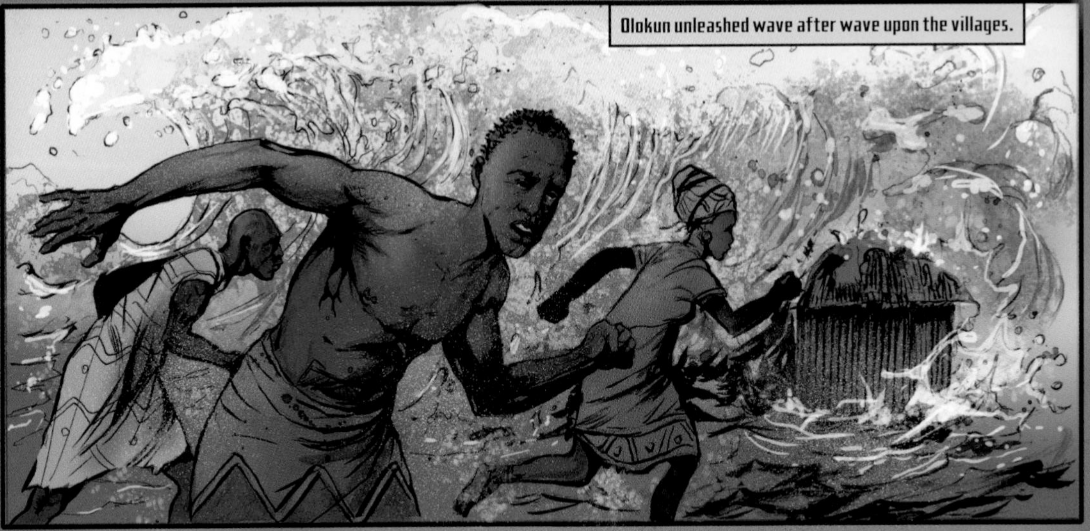
Olokun unleashed wave after wave upon the villages.

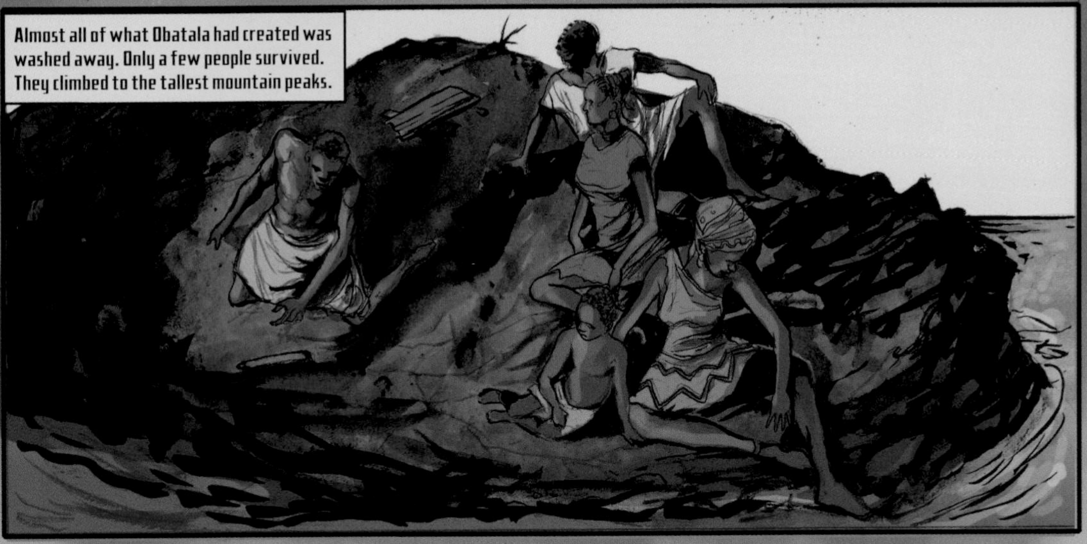
Almost all of what Obatala had created was washed away. Only a few people survived. They climbed to the tallest mountain peaks.

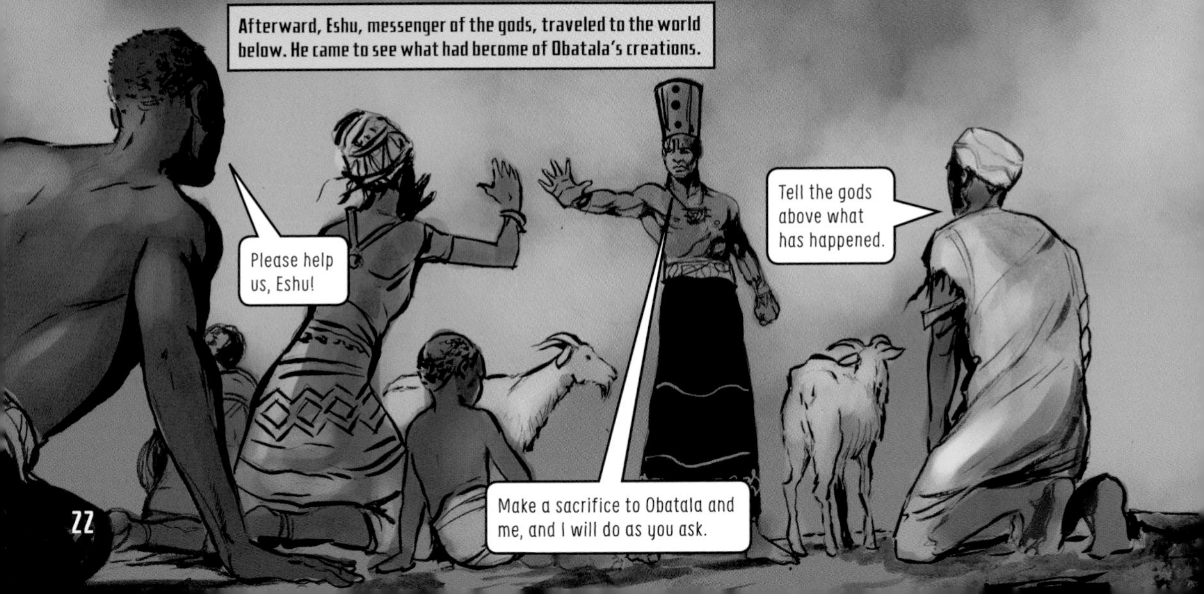
Afterward, Eshu, messenger of the gods, traveled to the world below. He came to see what had become of Obatala's creations.
Please help us, Eshu!
Tell the gods above what has happened.
Make a sacrifice to Obatala and me, and I will do as you ask.

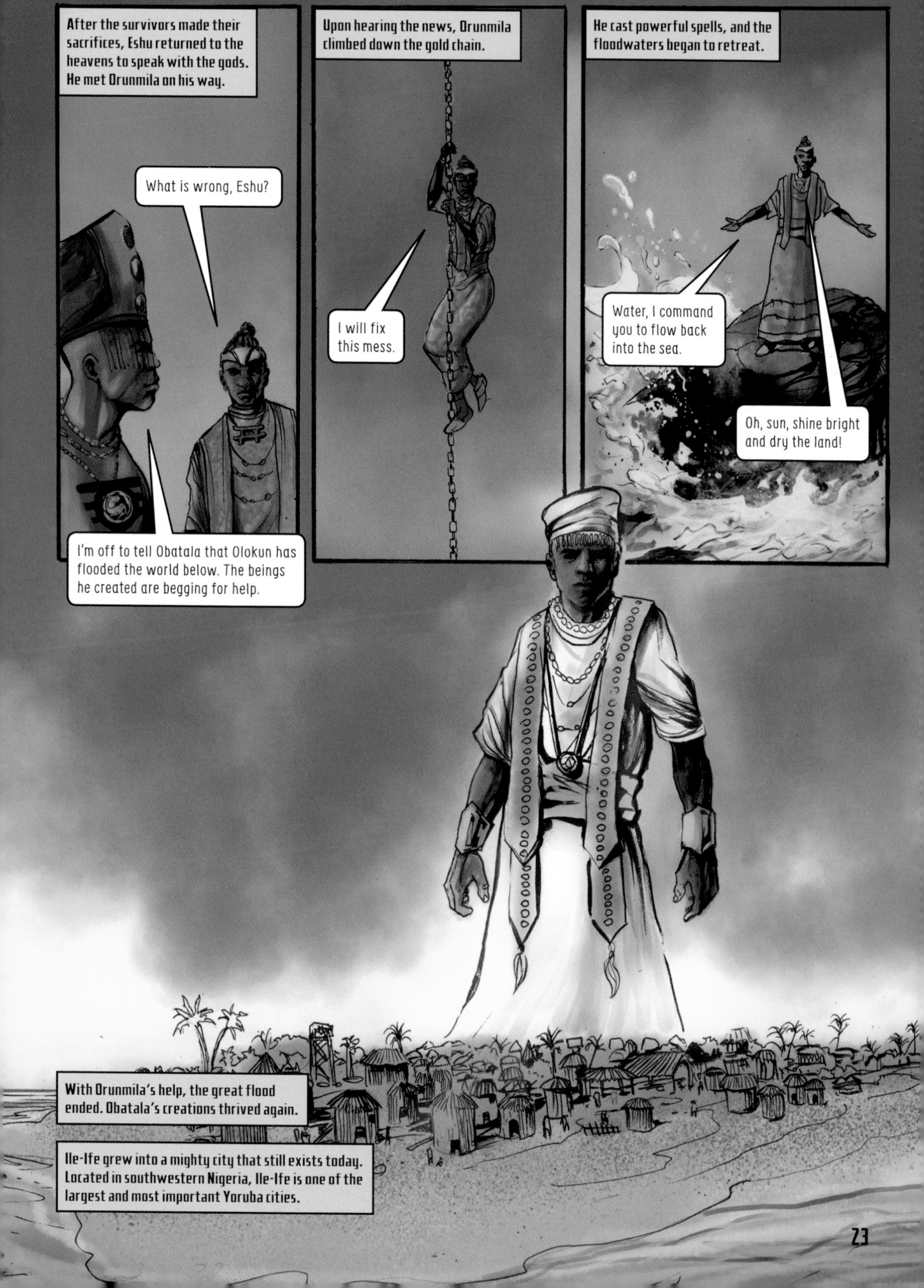
After the survivors made their sacrifices, Eshu returned to the heavens to speak with the gods. He met Orunmila on his way.
What is wrong, Eshu?
I'm off to tell Obatala that Olokun has flooded the world below. The beings he created are begging for help.
Upon hearing the news, Orunmila climbed down the gold chain.
I will fix this mess.
He cast powerful spells, and the floodwaters began to retreat.
Water, I command you to flow back into the sea.
Oh, sun, shine bright and dry the land!
With Orunmila's help, the great flood ended. Obatala's creations thrived again.
Ile-Ife grew into a mighty city that still exists today. Located in southwestern Nigeria, Ile-Ife is one of the largest and most important Yoruba cities.

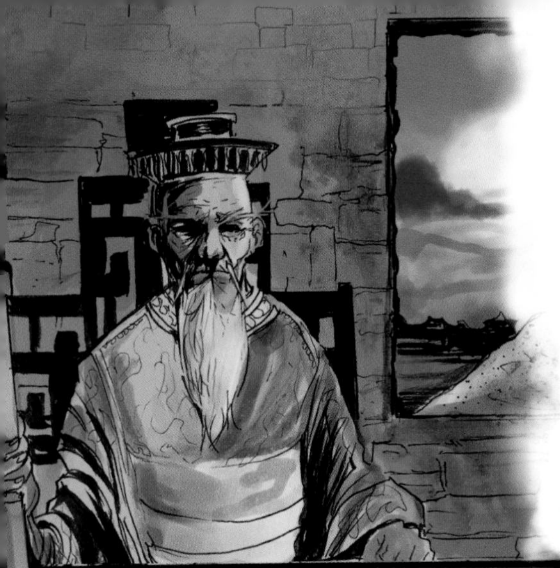

CHAPTER FOUR

THE YELLOW EMPEROR'S MAGICAL DIRT

A CHINESE MYTH

ANCIENT RULERS OF CHINA WERE OFTEN SEEN AS MYTHICAL GODS. ONE SUCH FIGURE WAS THE YELLOW EMPEROR. HE IS AT THE CENTER OF MANY CHINESE MYTHS, INCLUDING THIS FLOOD MYTH. UNLIKE OTHER CULTURES' STORIES OF DELUGES, THIS IS NOT A TALE OF DESTRUCTION. INSTEAD, IT IS ABOUT TAMING DEADLY FLOODING RIVERS.

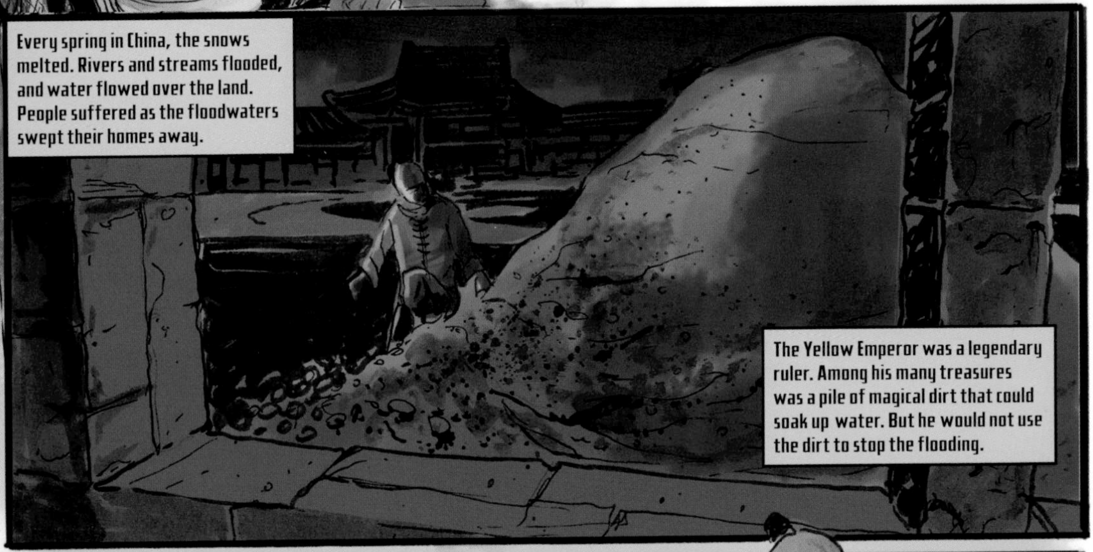
Every spring in China, the snows melted. Rivers and streams flooded, and water flowed over the land. People suffered as the floodwaters swept their homes away.
The Yellow Emperor was a legendary ruler. Among his many treasures was a pile of magical dirt that could soak up water. But he would not use the dirt to stop the flooding.

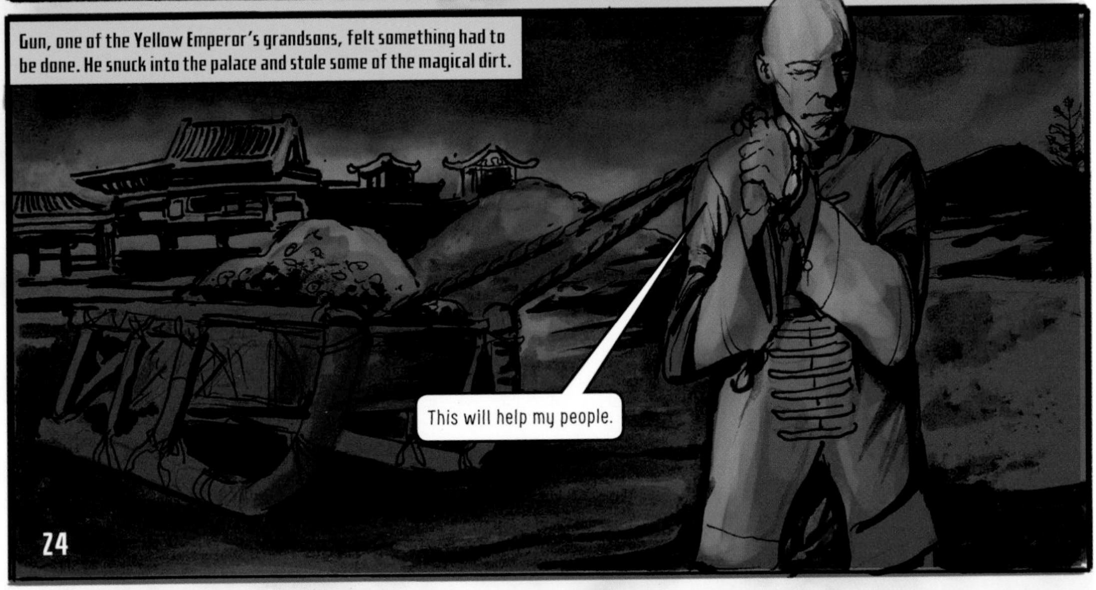
Gun, one of the Yellow Emperor's grandsons, felt something had to be done. He snuck into the palace and stole some of the magical dirt.
This will help my people.

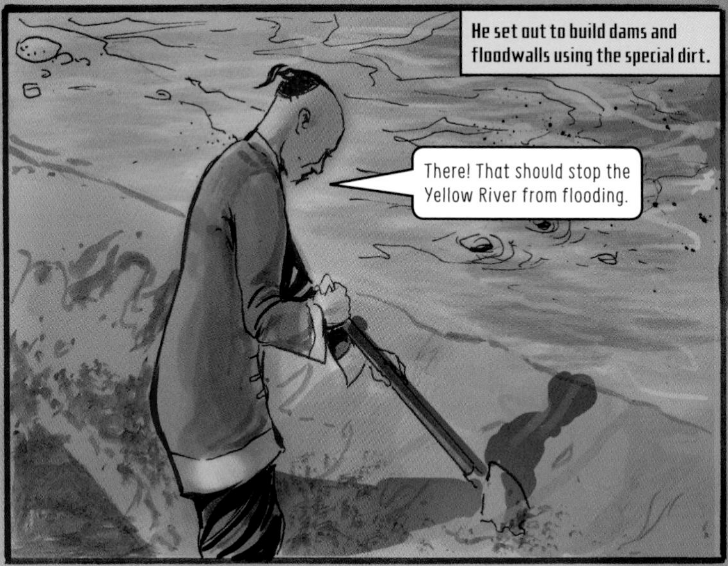
He set out to build dams and floodwalls using the special dirt.
There! That should stop the Yellow River from flooding.

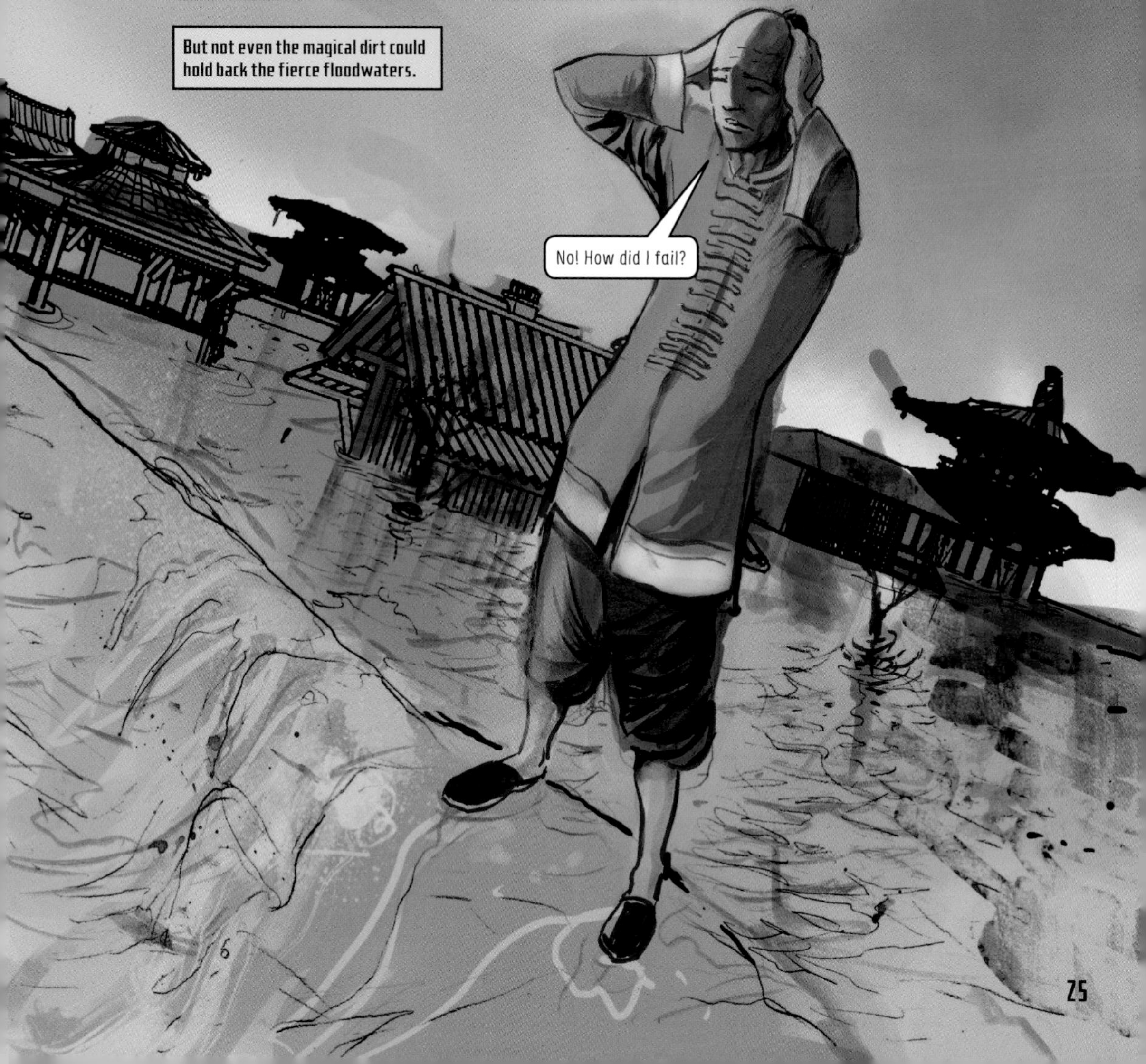
But not even the magical dirt could hold back the fierce floodwaters.
No! How did I fail?

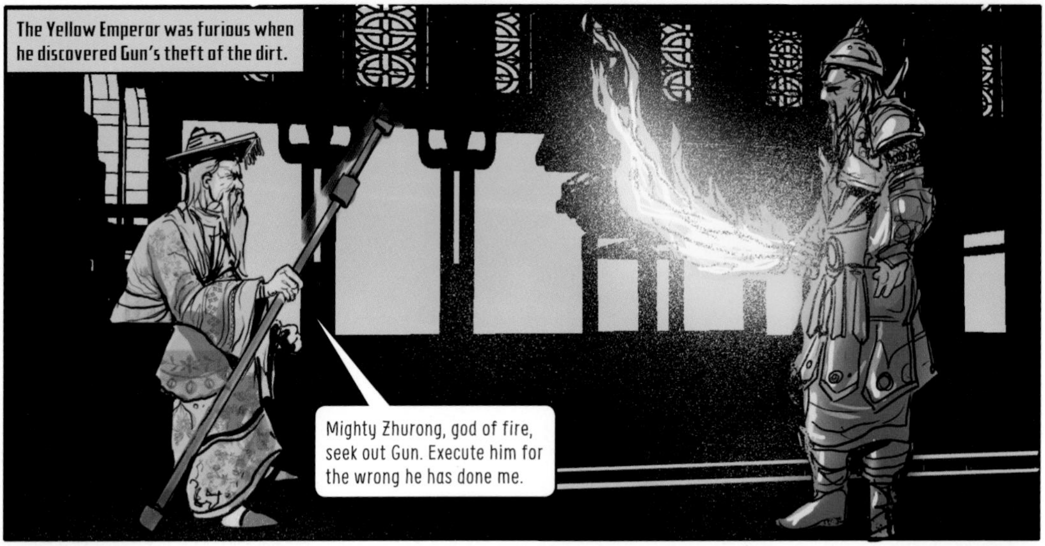
The Yellow Emperor was furious when he discovered Gun's theft of the dirt.
Mighty Zhurong, god of fire, seek out Gun. Execute him for the wrong he has done me.

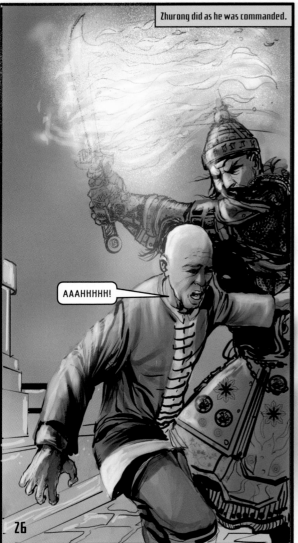

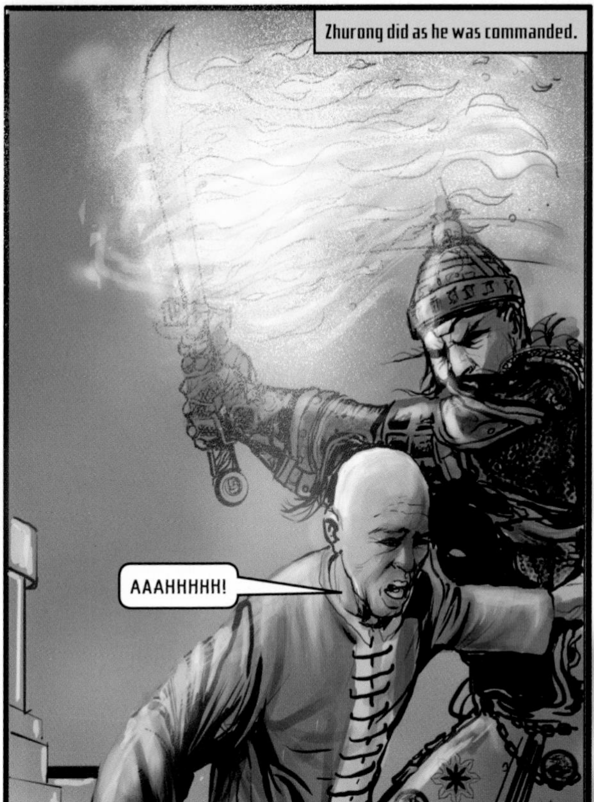
Zhurong did as he was commanded.
AAAHHHHH!

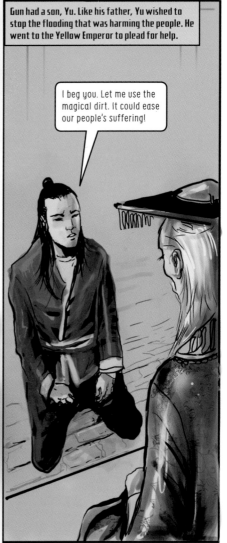

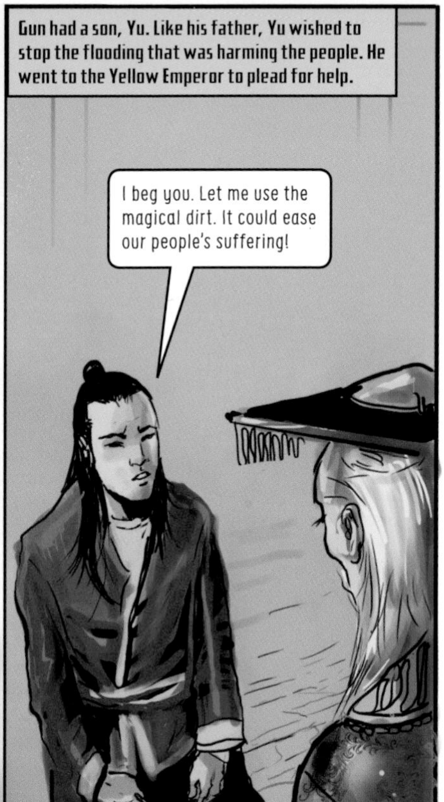
Gun had a son, Yu. Like his father, Yu wished to stop the flooding that was harming the people. He went to the Yellow Emperor to plead for help.
I beg you. Let me use the magical dirt. It could ease our people's suffering!

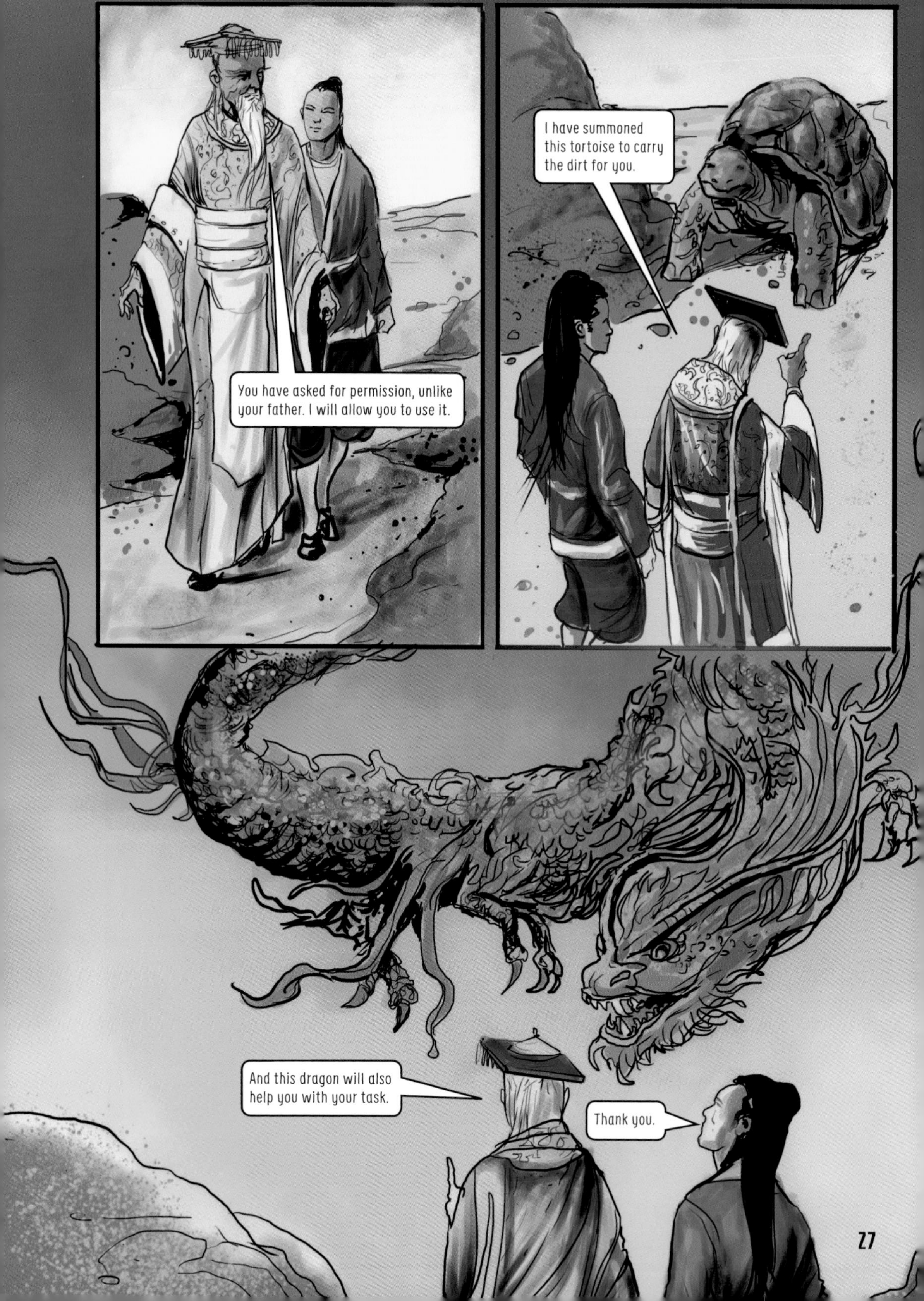
You have asked for permission, unlike your father. I will allow you to use it.
I have summoned this tortoise to carry the dirt for you.
And this dragon will also help you with your task.
Thank you.

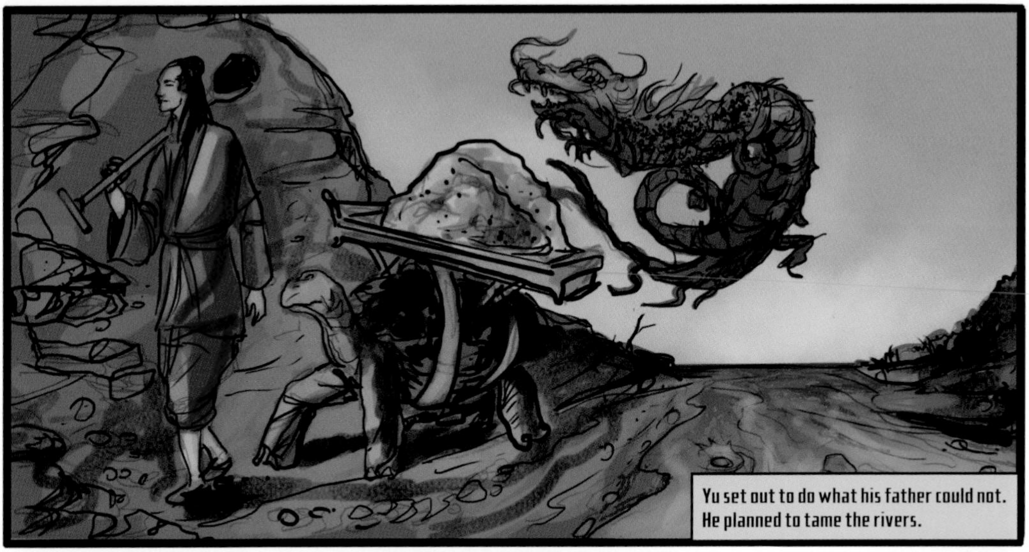
Yu set out to do what his father could not. He planned to tame the rivers.

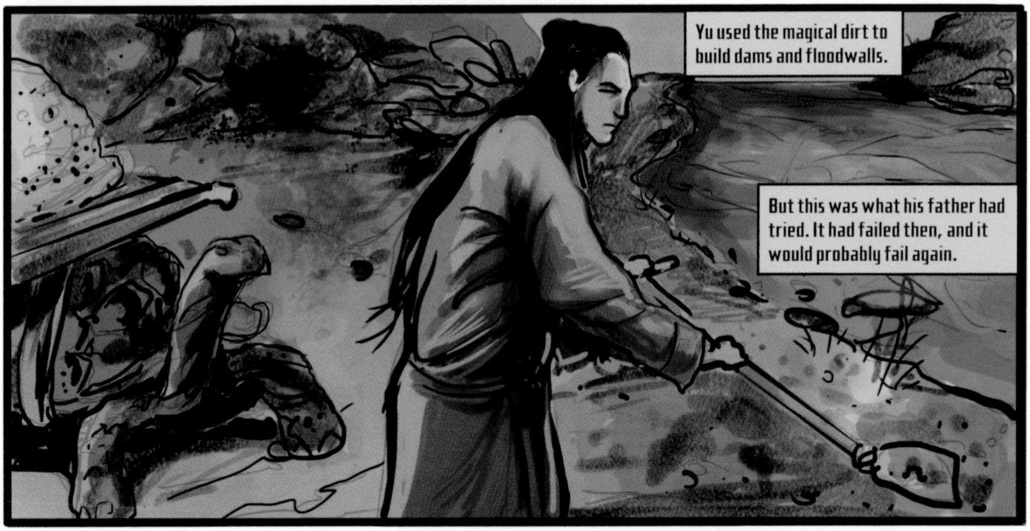
Yu used the magical dirt to build dams and floodwalls.
But this was what his father had tried. It had failed then, and it would probably fail again.

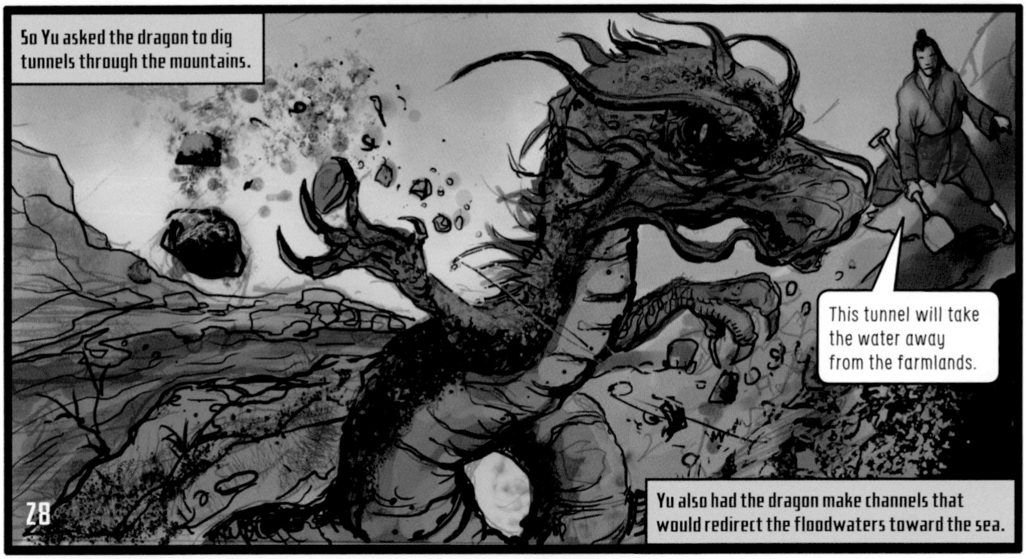
So Yu asked the dragon to dig tunnels through the mountains.
This tunnel will take the water away from the farmlands.
Yu also had the dragon make channels that would redirect the floodwaters toward the sea.

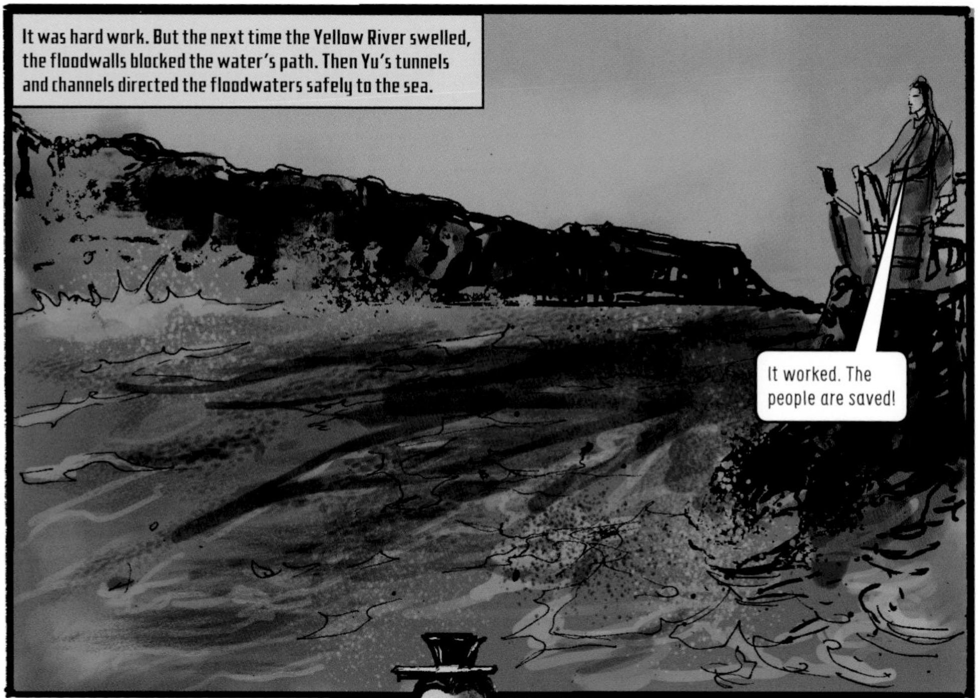
It was hard work. But the next time the Yellow River swelled, the floodwalls blocked the water's path. Then Yu's tunnels and channels directed the floodwaters safely to the sea.
It worked. The people are saved!

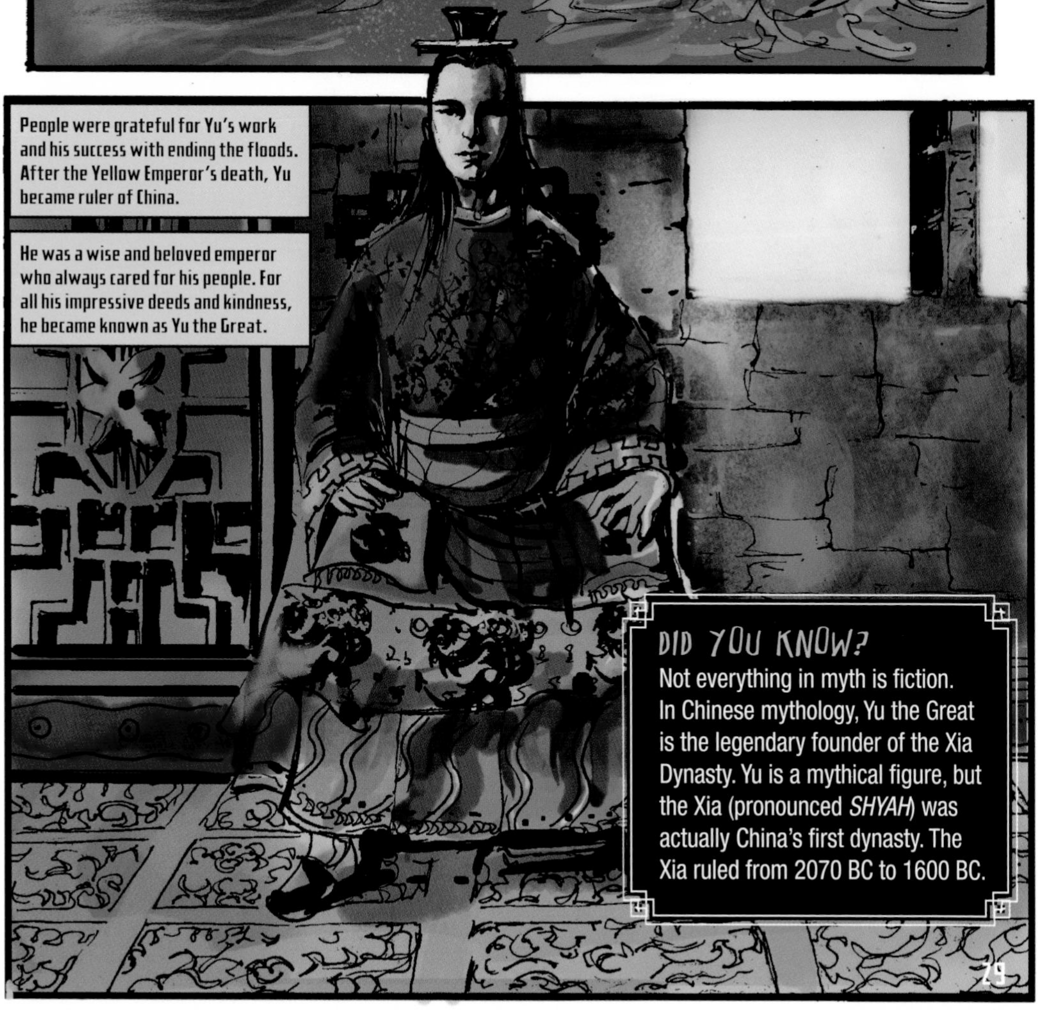
People were grateful for Yu's work and his success with ending the floods. After the Yellow Emperor's death, Yu became ruler of China.
He was a wise and beloved emperor who always cared for his people. For all his impressive deeds and kindness, he became known as Yu the Great.

DID YOU KNOW?

Not everything in myth is fiction. In Chinese mythology, Yu the Great is the legendary founder of the Xia Dynasty. Yu is a mythical figure, but the Xia (pronounced *SHYAH*) was actually China's first dynasty. The Xia ruled from 2070 BC to 1600 BC.

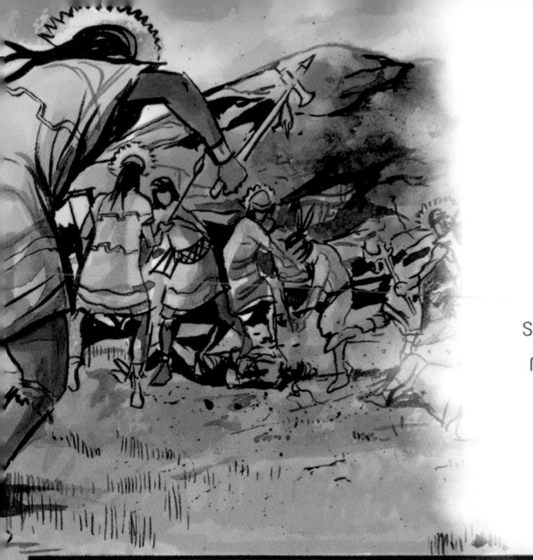

CHAPTER FIVE

TWO BROTHERS AND THEIR LLAMAS

AN INCAN MYTH

FROM THE 1100S TO THE 1500S, THE INCAS RULED MUCH OF SOUTH AMERICA. THEY HAD MANY FLOOD STORIES, AND IN THIS MYTH, THE INCAS TOLD OF A PERIOD CALLED PACHACHAMA. IT WAS A TIME WHEN PEOPLE WERE CRUEL AND DID NOT FEAR THE GODS. BUT THE GODS WERE WATCHING, AND THEY WERE PLANNING TO RID THE WORLD OF ITS WICKEDNESS . . .

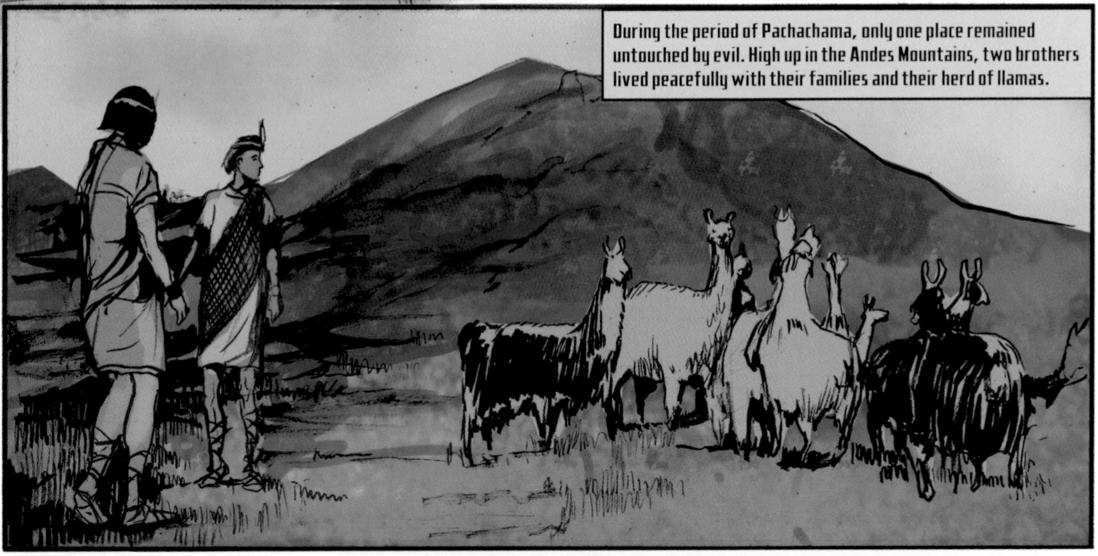
During the period of Pachachama, only one place remained untouched by evil. High up in the Andes Mountains, two brothers lived peacefully with their families and their herd of llamas.

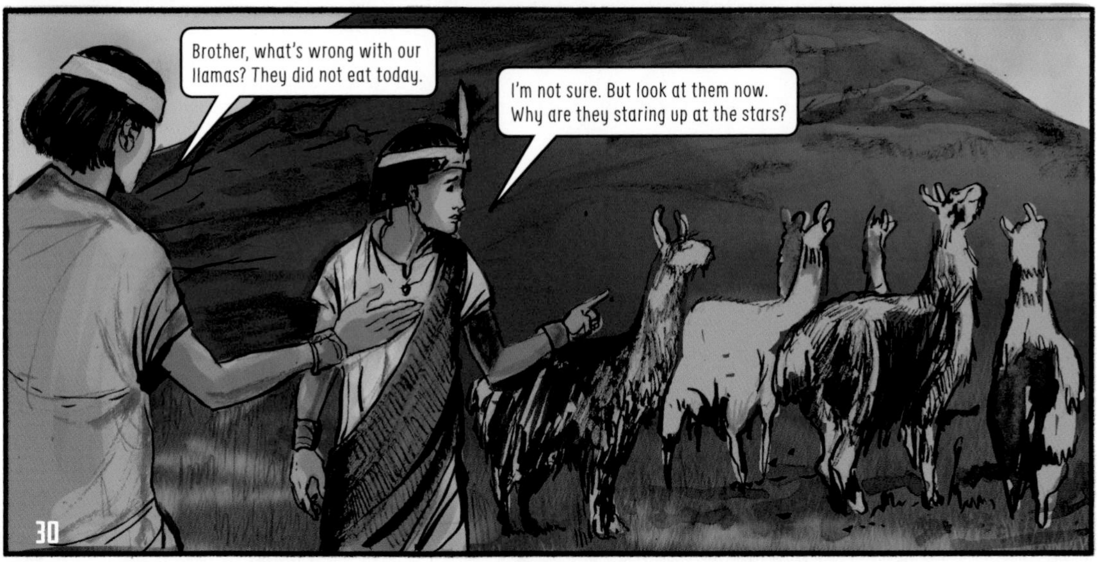
Brother, what's wrong with our llamas? They did not eat today.
I'm not sure. But look at them now. Why are they staring up at the stars?

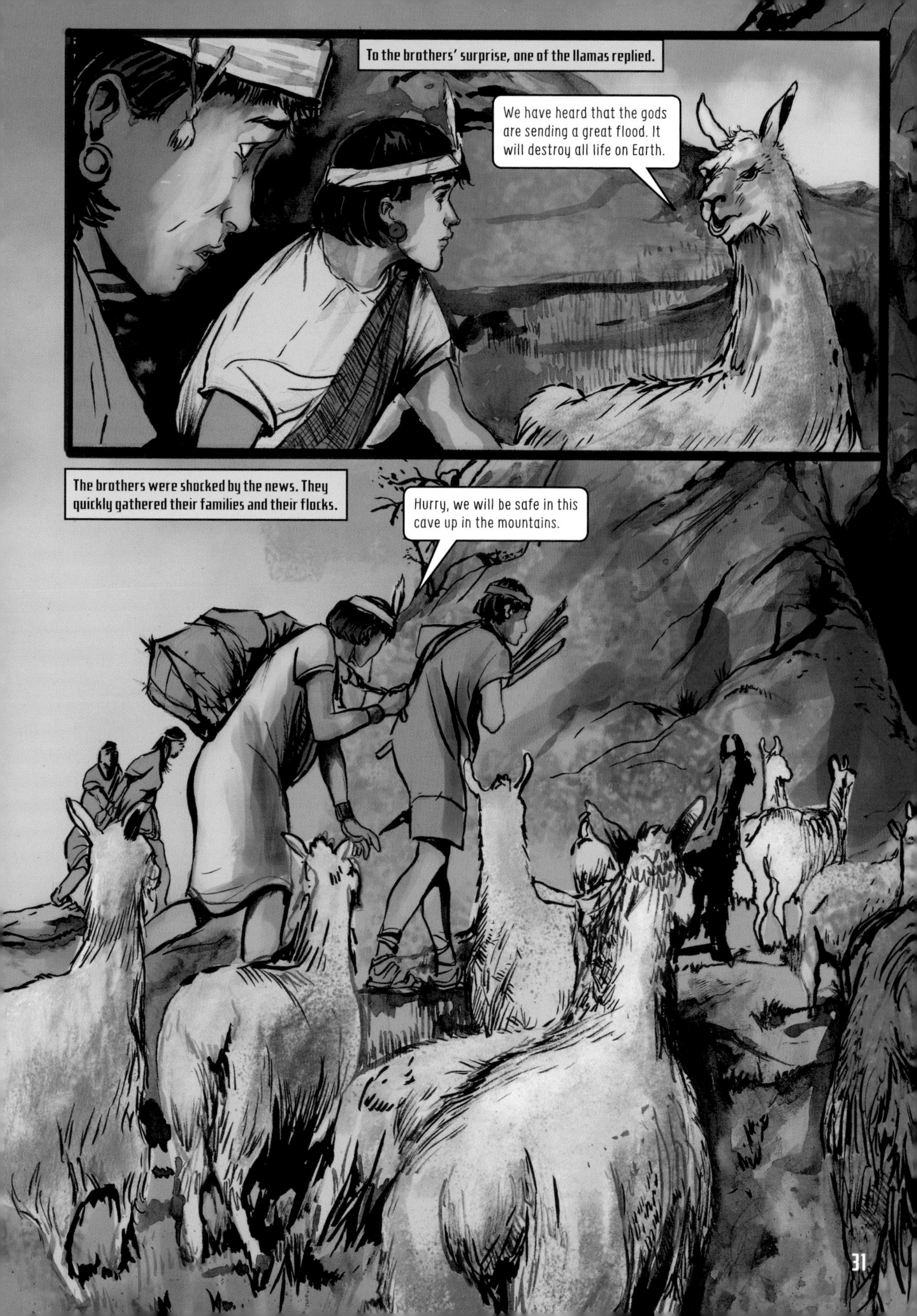
To the brothers' surprise, one of the llamas replied.
We have heard that the gods are sending a great flood. It will destroy all life on Earth.
The brothers were shocked by the news. They quickly gathered their families and their flocks.
Hurry, we will be safe in this cave up in the mountains.

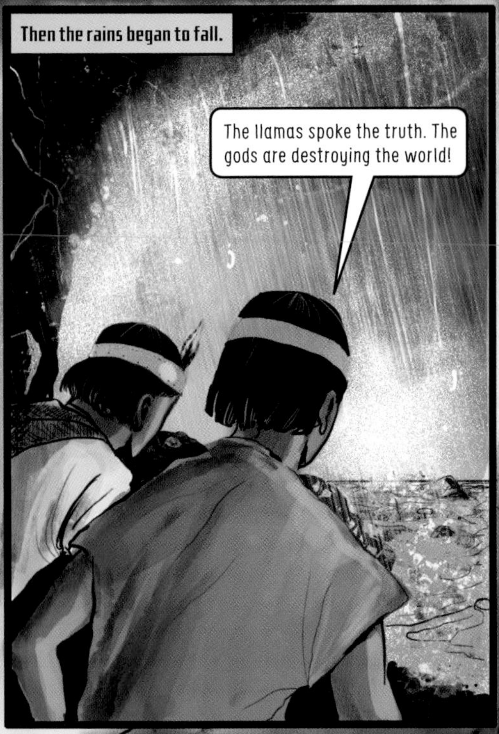
Then the rains began to fall.
The llamas spoke the truth. The gods are destroying the world!

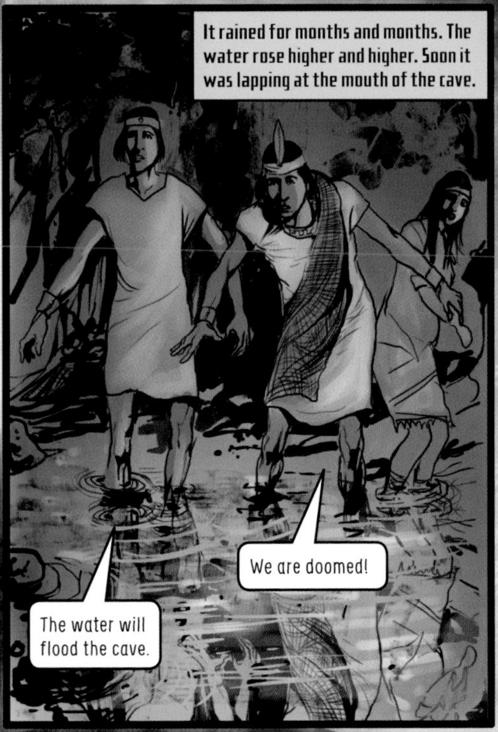
It rained for months and months. The water rose higher and higher. Soon it was lapping at the mouth of the cave.
The water will flood the cave.
We are doomed!

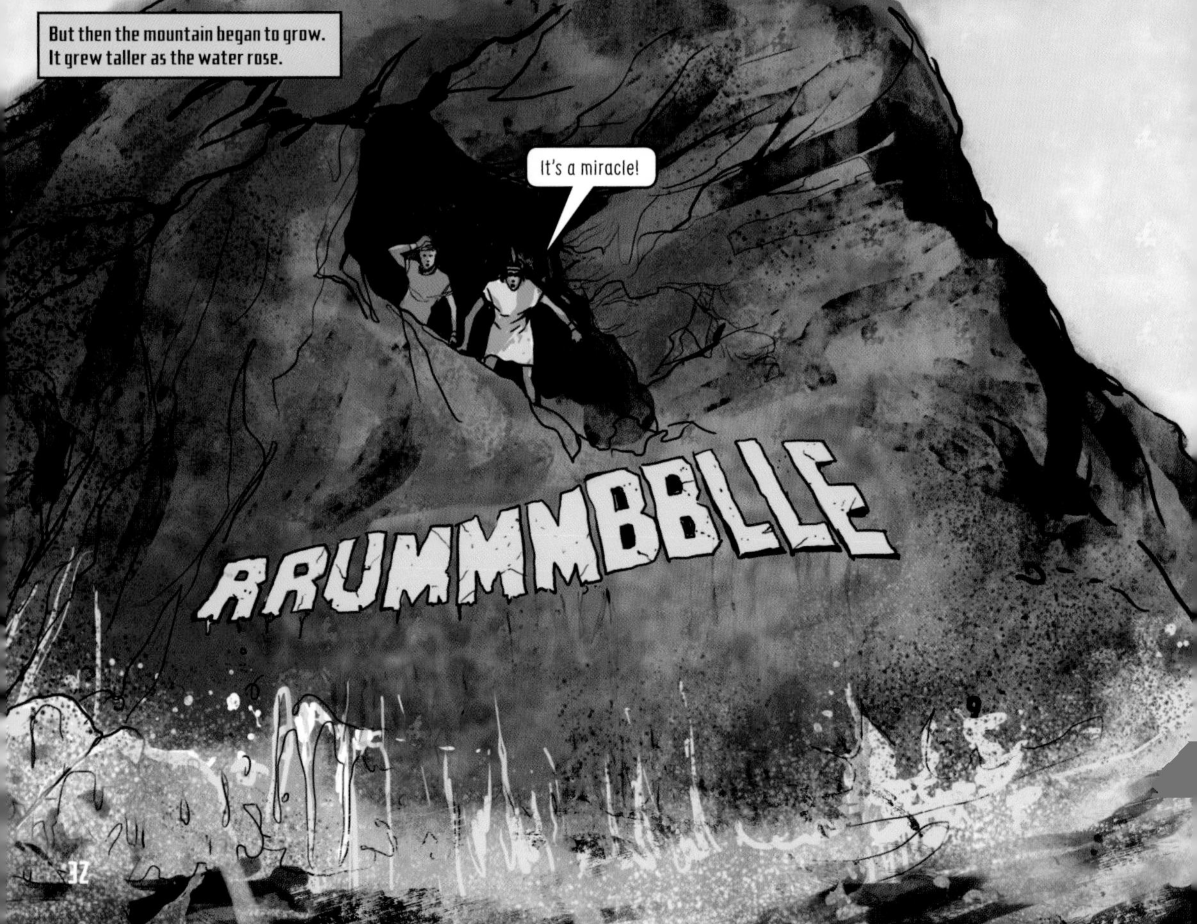
But then the mountain began to grow. It grew taller as the water rose.
It's a miracle!
RRUMMMBBLLE

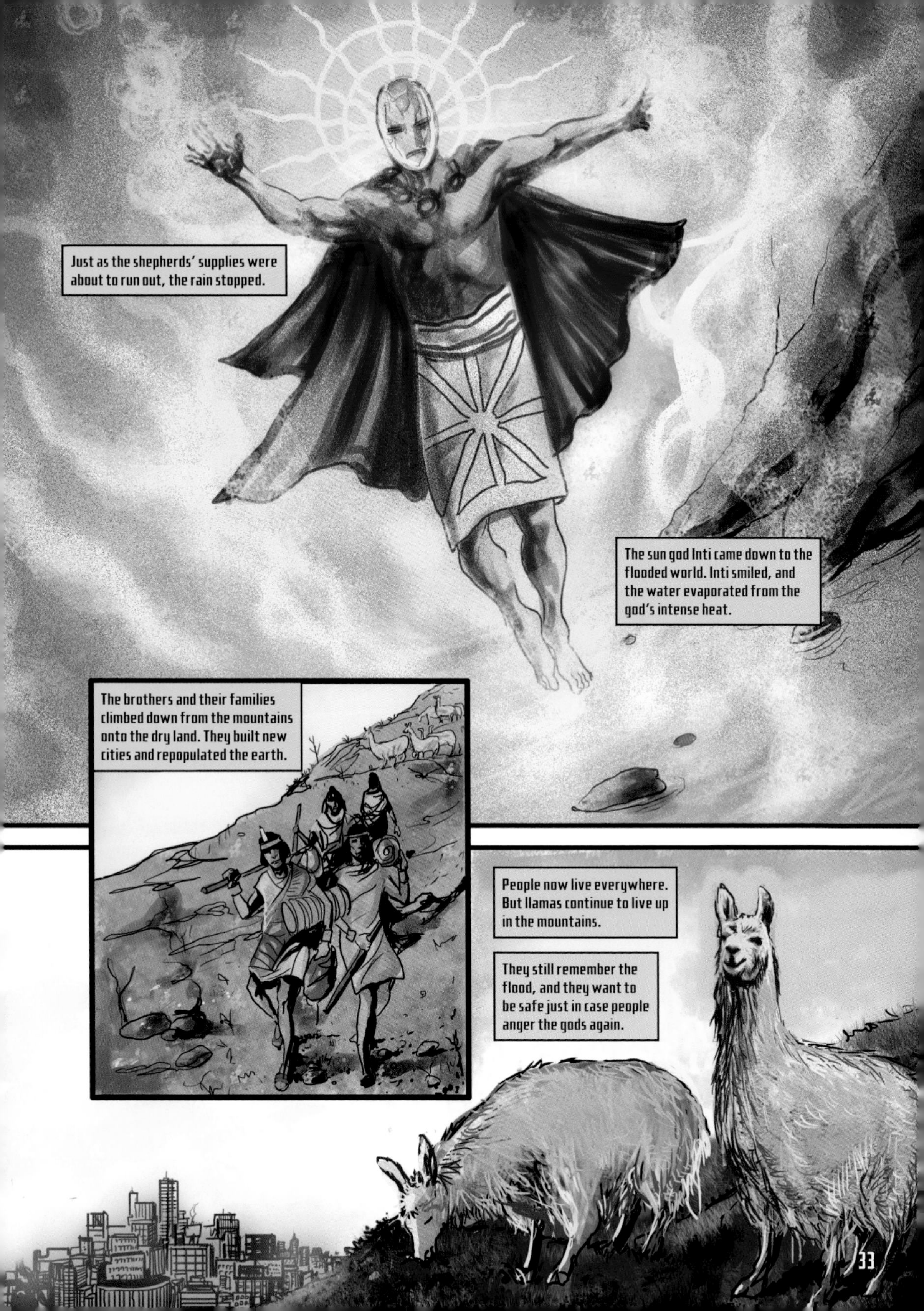

Just as the shepherds' supplies were about to run out, the rain stopped.
The sun god Inti came down to the flooded world. Inti smiled, and the water evaporated from the god's intense heat.
The brothers and their families climbed down from the mountains onto the dry land. They built new cities and repopulated the earth.
People now live everywhere. But llamas continue to live up in the mountains.
They still remember the flood, and they want to be safe just in case people anger the gods again.

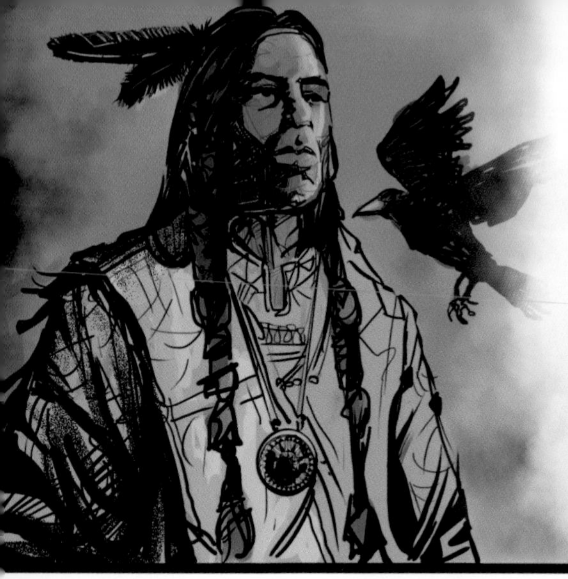

CHAPTER SIX

CROW AND TURTLE

A LAKOTA MYTH

IN MANY NATIVE AMERICAN MYTHS, IT IS SAID OTHER WORLDS EXISTED BEFORE THIS ONE. THOSE WORLDS WERE IMPERFECT, SO THE CREATING SPIRIT DESTROYED THEM IN ORDER TO MAKE A BETTER ONE. IN THE CASE OF THIS LAKOTA LEGEND, ALL WAS NOT SWEPT AWAY IN THE FLOOD. A CROW SURVIVED THE VIOLENT WATERS. WITH THE URGING OF THE BIRD AND HELP FROM A TALENTED TURTLE, THE SPIRIT WAKAN TANKA (**WAH**-KAHN **TAHN**-KAH) MADE THE WORLD WHOLE AGAIN.

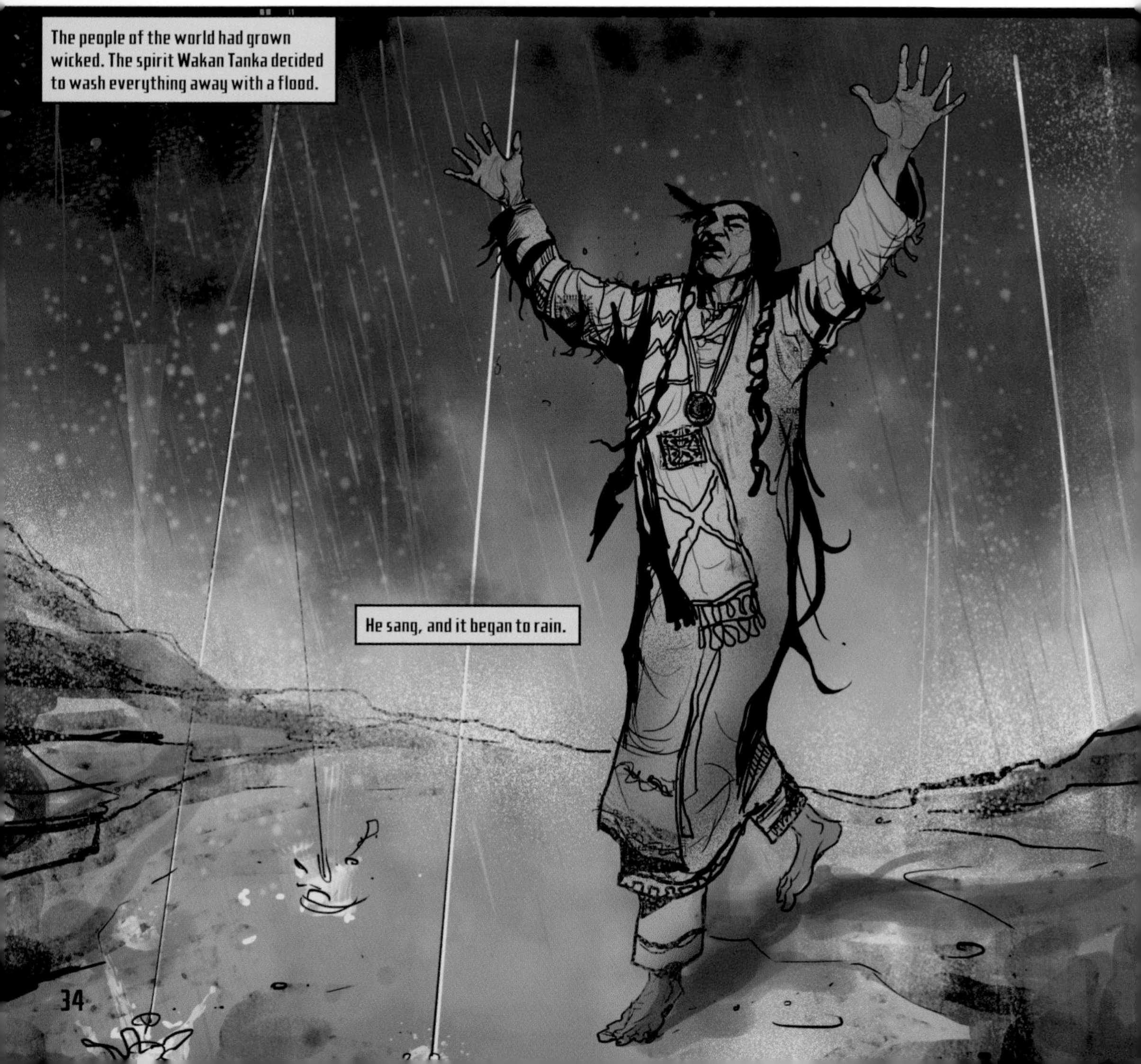
The people of the world had grown wicked. The spirit Wakan Tanka decided to wash everything away with a flood.
He sang, and it began to rain.

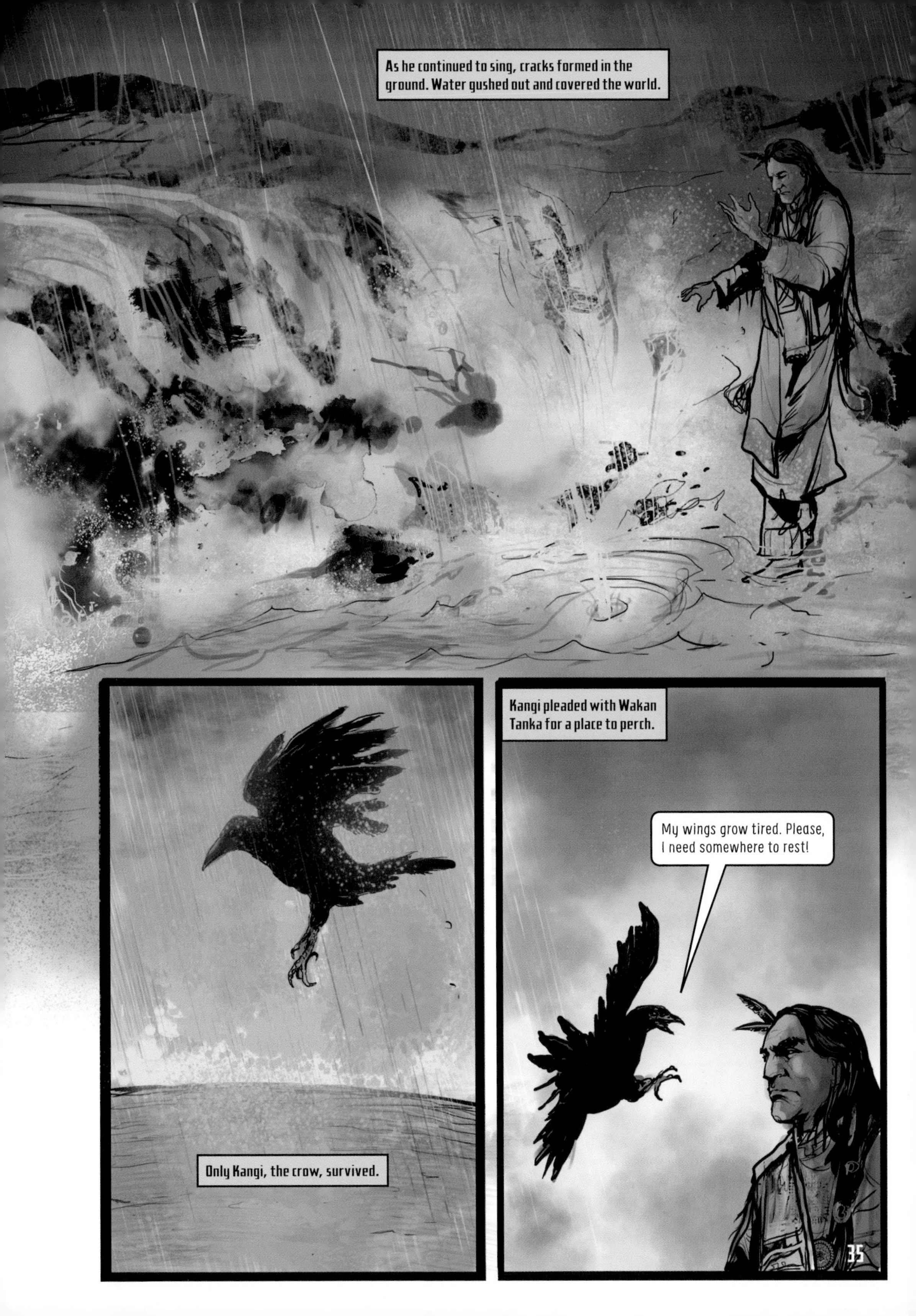

As he continued to sing, cracks formed in the ground. Water gushed out and covered the world.
Only Kangi, the crow, survived.
Kangi pleaded with Wakan Tanka for a place to perch.
My wings grow tired. Please, I need somewhere to rest!

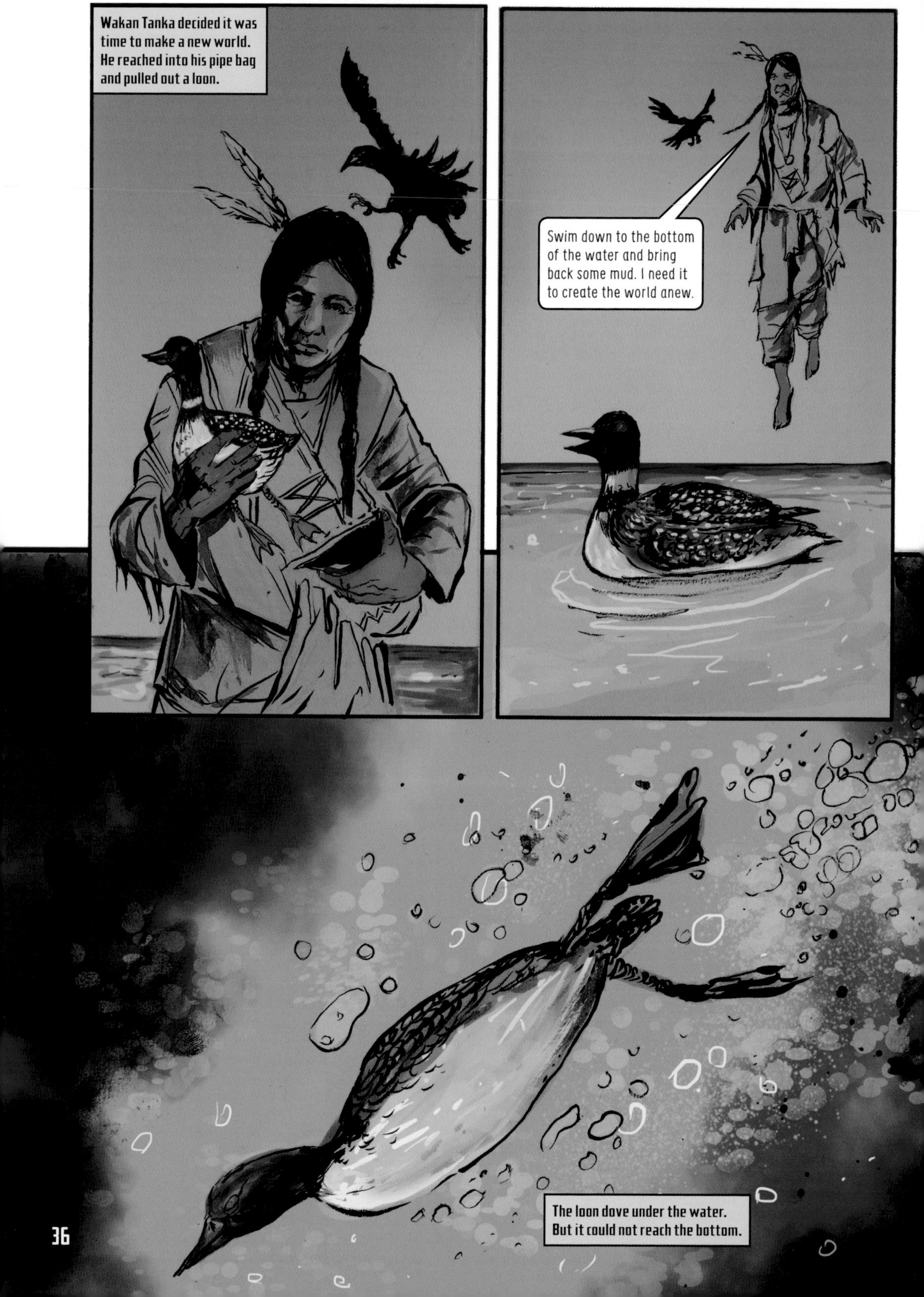

Wakan Tanka decided it was time to make a new world. He reached into his pipe bag and pulled out a loon.
Swim down to the bottom of the water and bring back some mud. I need it to create the world anew.
The loon dove under the water. But it could not reach the bottom.

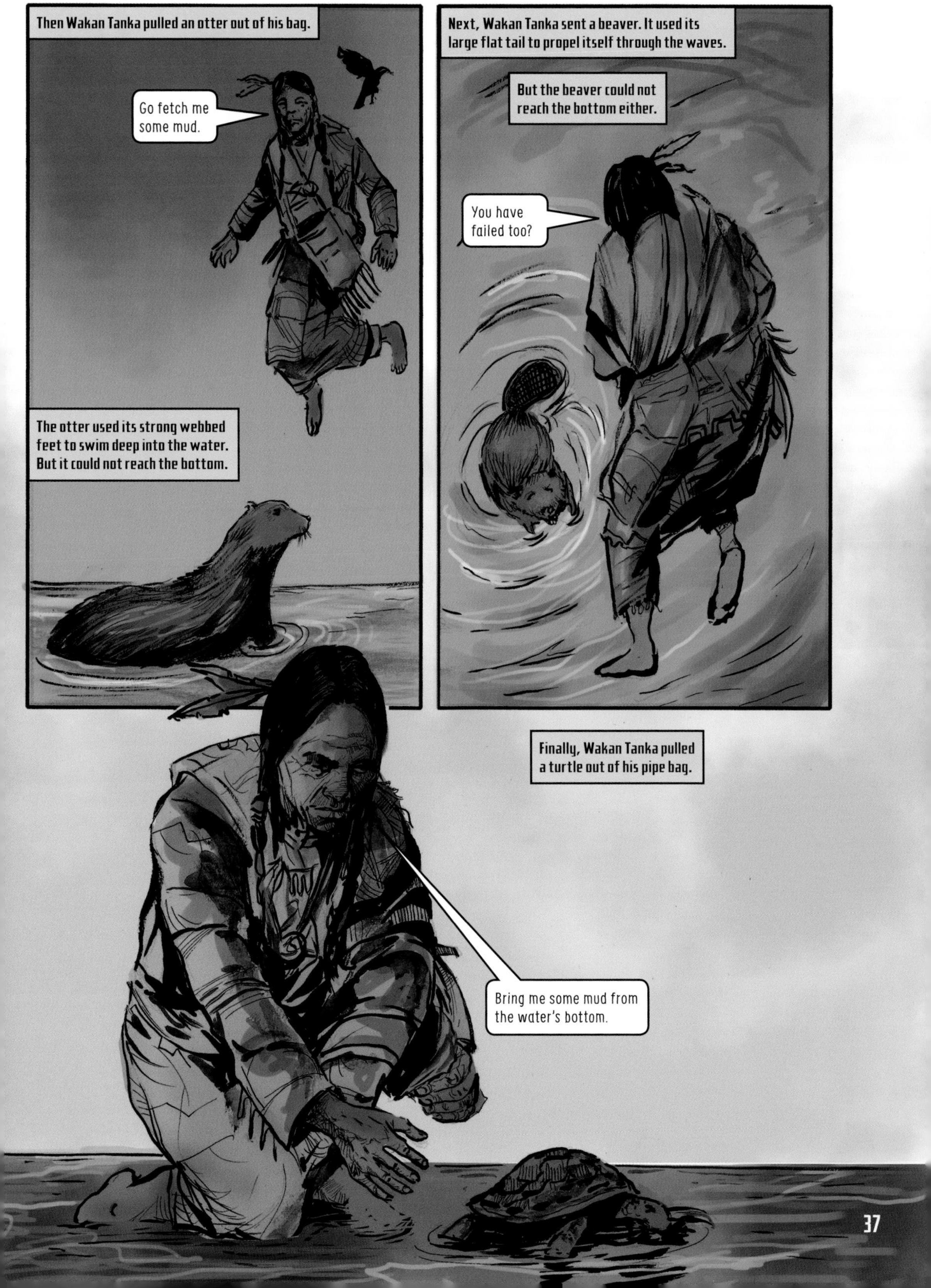

Then Wakan Tanka pulled an otter out of his bag.
Go fetch me some mud.
The otter used its strong webbed feet to swim deep into the water. But it could not reach the bottom.
Next, Wakan Tanka sent a beaver. It used its large flat tail to propel itself through the waves.
But the beaver could not reach the bottom either.
You have failed too?
Finally, Wakan Tanka pulled a turtle out of his pipe bag.
Bring me some mud from the water's bottom.

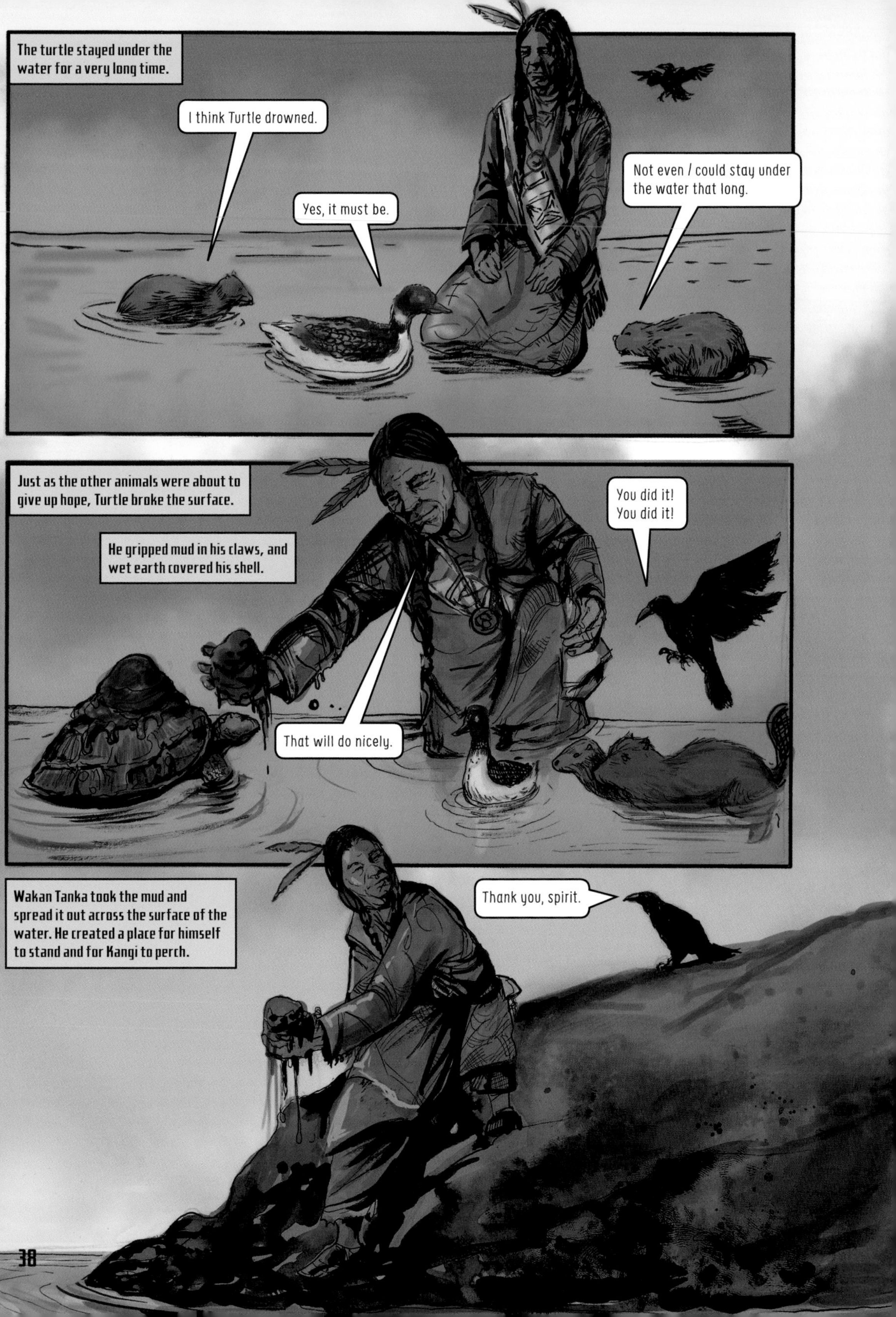

The turtle stayed under the water for a very long time.
I think Turtle drowned.
Yes, it must be.
Not even I could stay under the water that long.
Just as the other animals were about to give up hope, Turtle broke the surface.
He gripped mud in his claws, and wet earth covered his shell.
You did it! You did it!
That will do nicely.
Wakan Tanka took the mud and spread it out across the surface of the water. He created a place for himself to stand and for Kangi to perch.
Thank you, spirit.

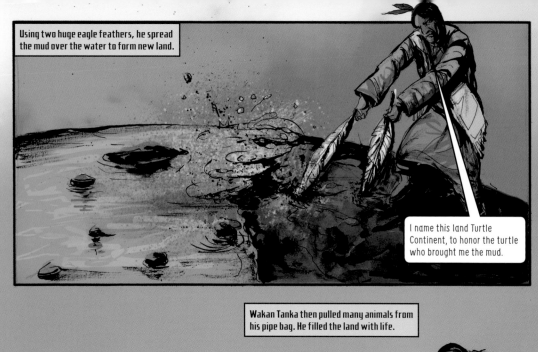

Using two huge eagle feathers, he spread the mud over the water to form new land.

I name this land Turtle Continent, to honor the turtle who brought me the mud.

Wakan Tanka then pulled many animals from his pipe bag. He filled the land with life.

Lastly, he pulled out people from his pipe bag. Wakan Tanka gave the new humans his sacred pipe.

Let this pipe remind you of the people that came before you. Live in peace and harmony and all will be well. But if you do not, I will end your world like I did theirs.

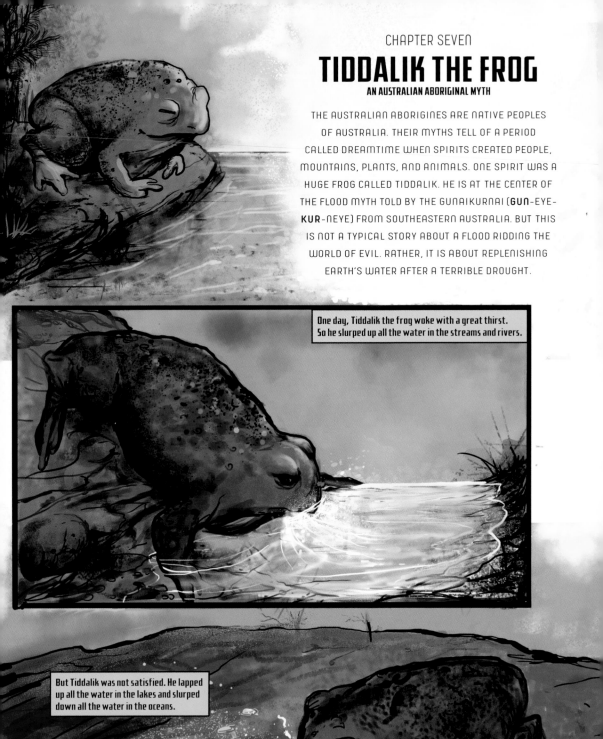

CHAPTER SEVEN

TIDDALIK THE FROG

AN AUSTRALIAN ABORIGINAL MYTH

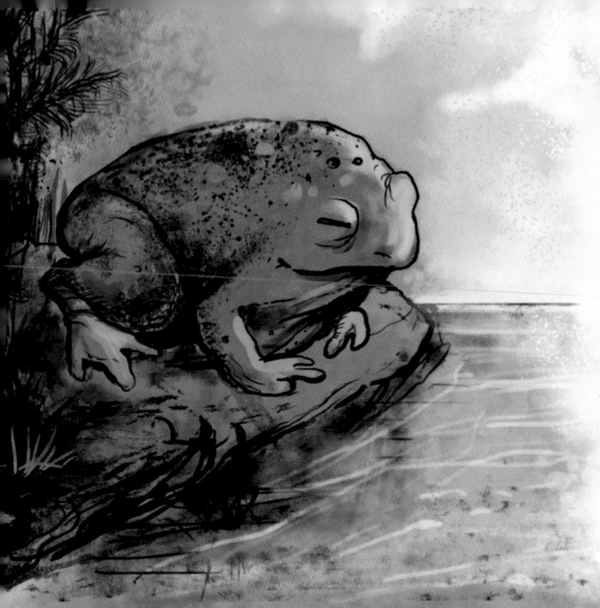

THE AUSTRALIAN ABORIGINES ARE NATIVE PEOPLES OF AUSTRALIA. THEIR MYTHS TELL OF A PERIOD CALLED DREAMTIME WHEN SPIRITS CREATED PEOPLE, MOUNTAINS, PLANTS, AND ANIMALS. ONE SPIRIT WAS A HUGE FROG CALLED TIDDALIK. HE IS AT THE CENTER OF THE FLOOD MYTH TOLD BY THE GUNAIKURNAI (**GUN**-EYE-**KUR**-NEYE) FROM SOUTHEASTERN AUSTRALIA. BUT THIS IS NOT A TYPICAL STORY ABOUT A FLOOD RIDDING THE WORLD OF EVIL. RATHER, IT IS ABOUT REPLENISHING EARTH'S WATER AFTER A TERRIBLE DROUGHT.

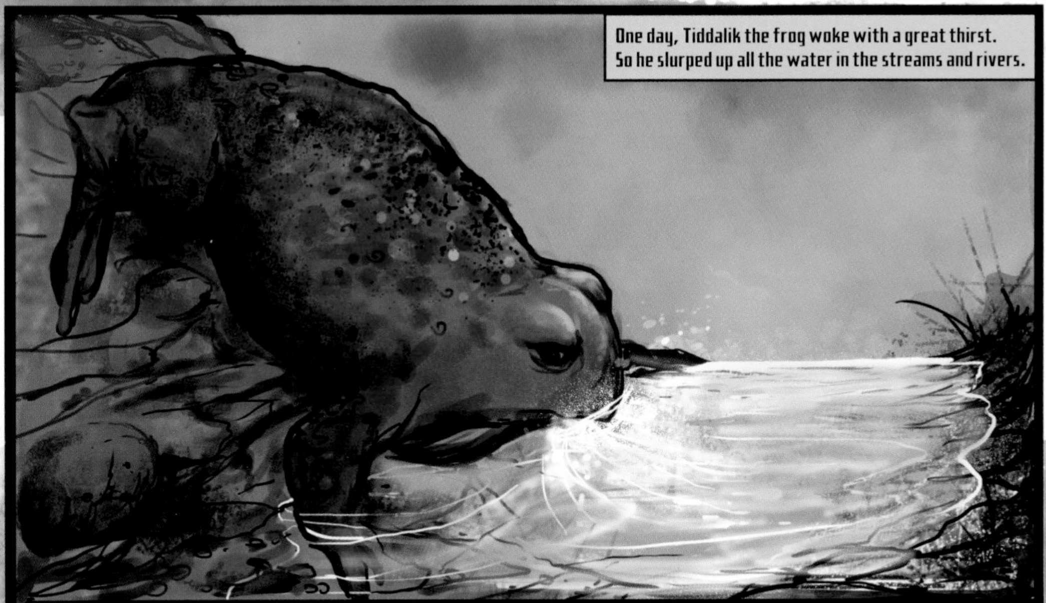
One day, Tiddalik the frog woke with a great thirst. So he slurped up all the water in the streams and rivers.

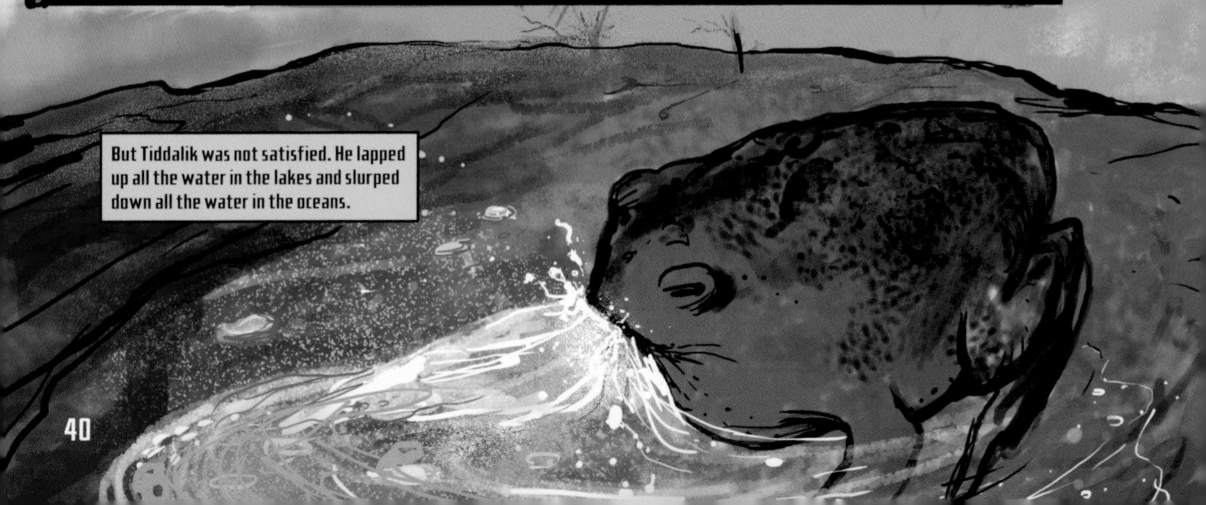
But Tiddalik was not satisfied. He lapped up all the water in the lakes and slurped down all the water in the oceans.

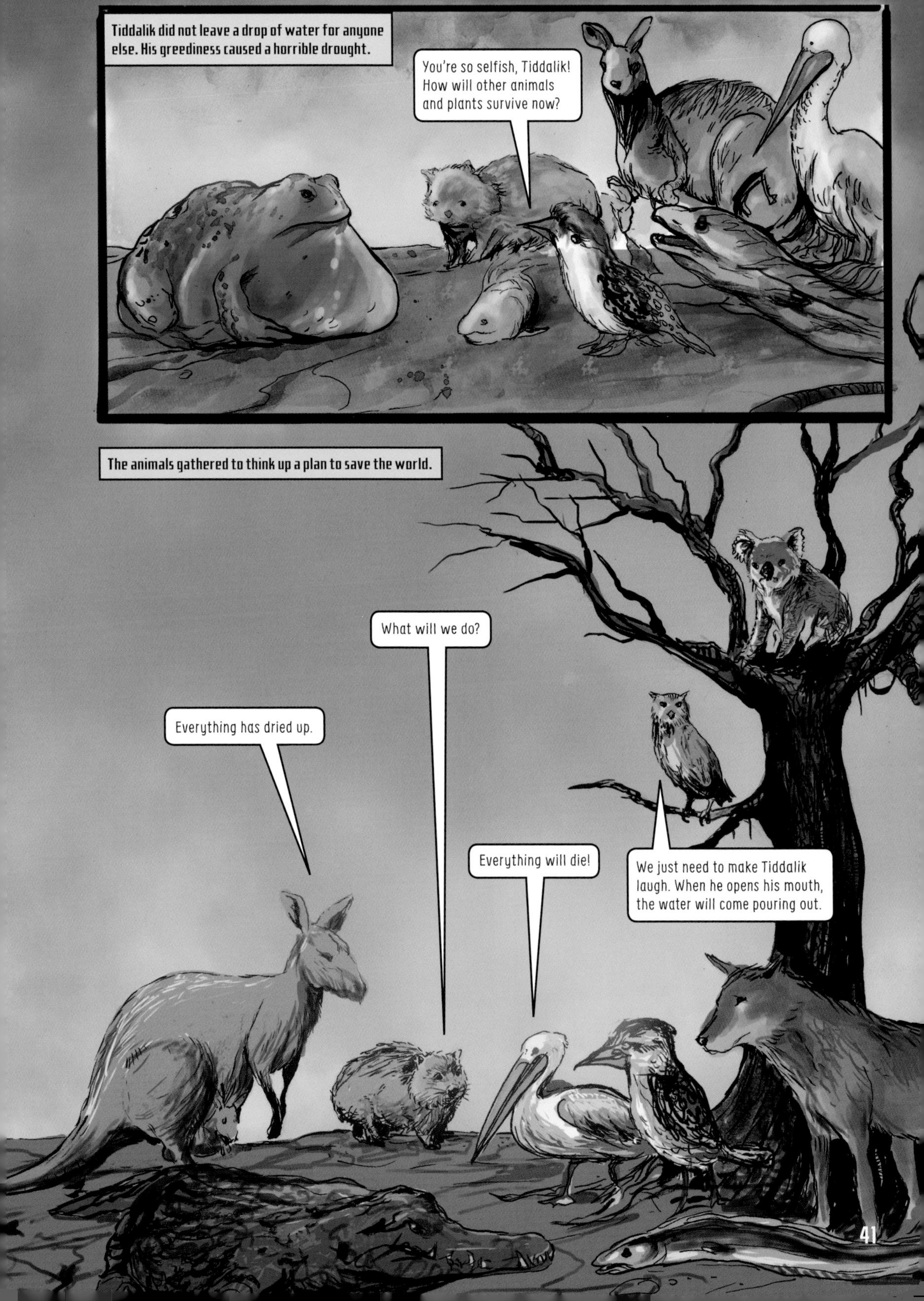
Tiddalik did not leave a drop of water for anyone else. His greediness caused a horrible drought.
You're so selfish, Tiddalik! How will other animals and plants survive now?
The animals gathered to think up a plan to save the world.
What will we do?
Everything has dried up.
Everything will die!
We just need to make Tiddalik laugh. When he opens his mouth, the water will come pouring out.

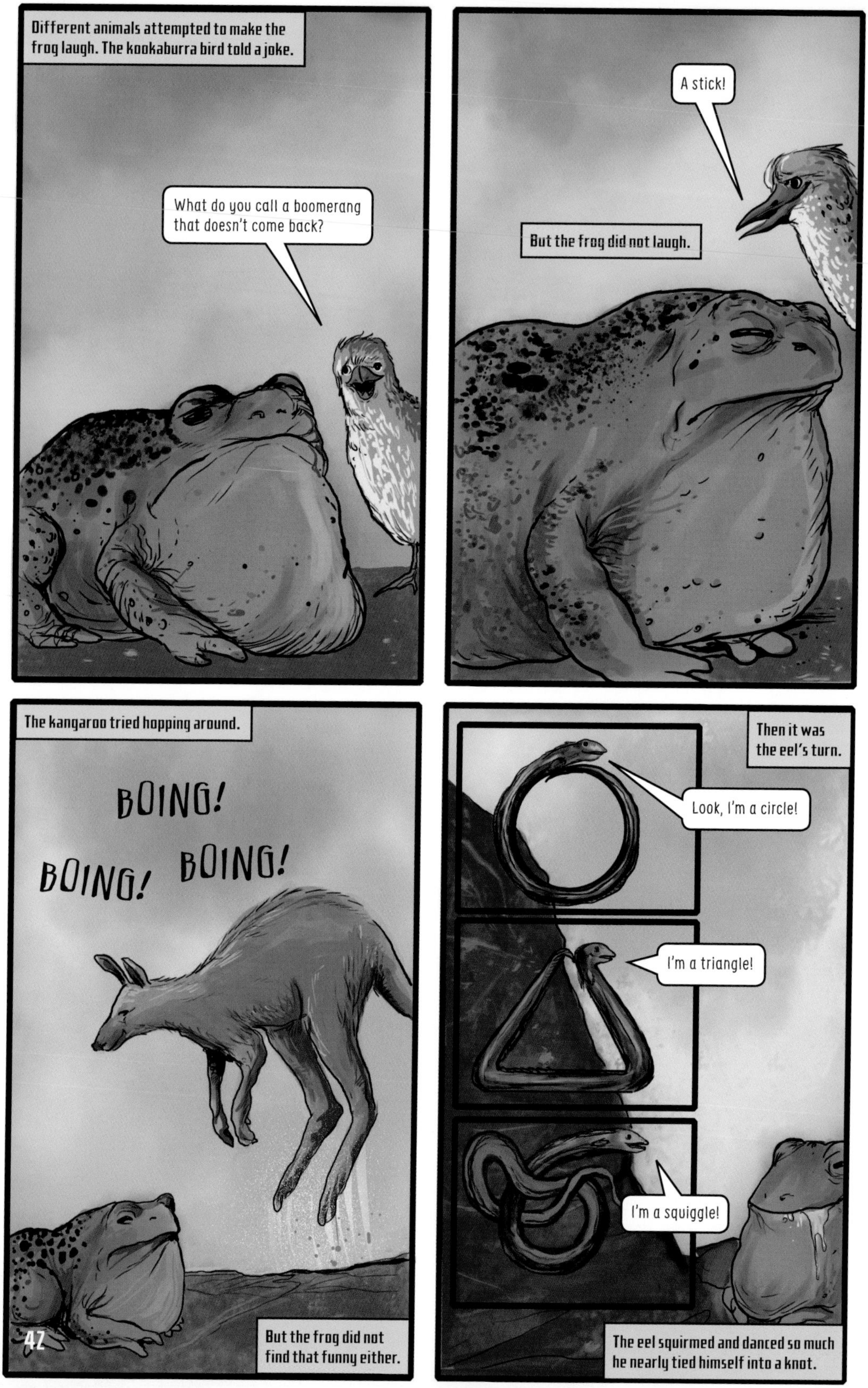
Different animals attempted to make the frog laugh. The kookaburra bird told a joke.
What do you call a boomerang that doesn't come back?
A stick!
But the frog did not laugh.
The kangaroo tried hopping around.
BOING!
BOING! BOING!
But the frog did not find that funny either.
Then it was the eel's turn.
Look, I'm a circle!
I'm a triangle!
I'm a squiggle!
The eel squirmed and danced so much he nearly tied himself into a knot.

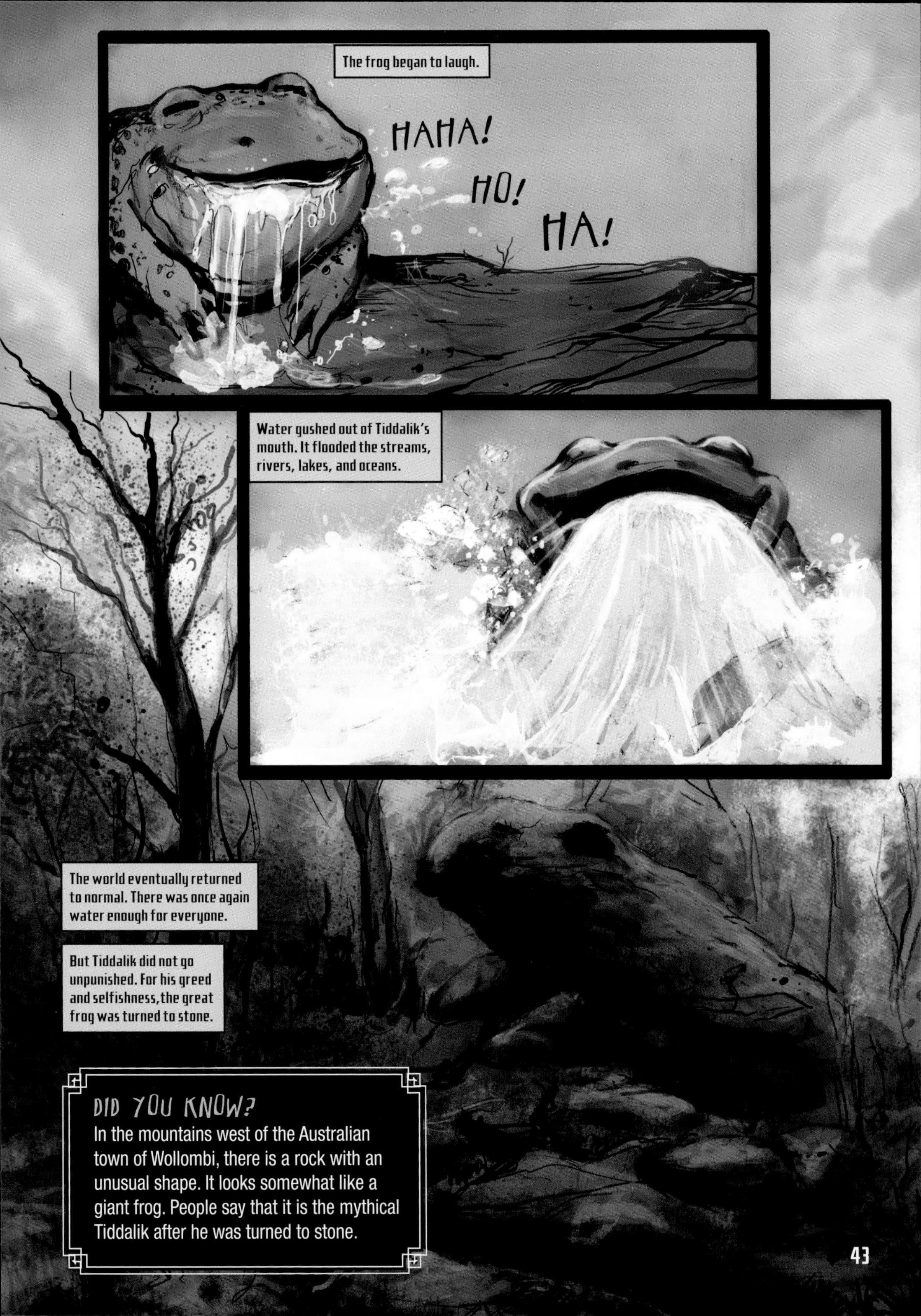
The frog began to laugh.
HAHA!
HO!
HA!
Water gushed out of Tiddalik's mouth. It flooded the streams, rivers, lakes, and oceans.
The world eventually returned to normal. There was once again water enough for everyone.
But Tiddalik did not go unpunished. For his greed and selfishness, the great frog was turned to stone.
DID YOU KNOW?
In the mountains west of the Australian town of Wollombi, there is a rock with an unusual shape. It looks somewhat like a giant frog. People say that it is the mythical Tiddalik after he was turned to stone.

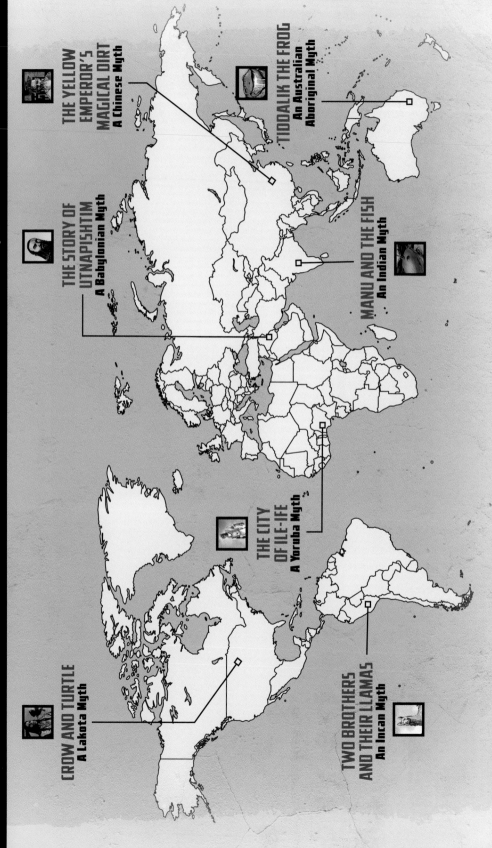

MYTH MAP AND MORE

THE YELLOW EMPEROR'S MAGICAL DIRT
A Chinese Myth

TIDDALIK THE FROG
An Australian Aboriginal Myth

THE STORY OF UTNAPISHTIM
A Babylonian Myth

MANU AND THE FISH
An Indian Myth

CROW AND TURTLE
A Lakota Myth

THE CITY OF ILE-IFE
A Yoruba Myth

TWO BROTHERS AND THEIR LLAMAS
An Incan Myth

- Way back in 2800 BC, the Euphrates River swelled to flood a large portion of Mesopotamia. This catastrophic event is one possible source for myths of a great flood. Other theories say the myths are based on terrible flooding that occurred after the last ice age.

- The Sumerian text *Eridu Genesis* contains the first known story of a great flood. It was written on stone tablets more than 4,000 years ago. Most of the tablets have been destroyed, so we do not know the full text of *Eridu Genesis*. But its tale of a terrible flood has influenced many other flood stories. Much of the *Epic of Gilgamesh* is based on *Eridu Genesis*.

- The Yellow Emperor is one of China's legendary rulers. His rule is said to have begun in 2697 BC and lasted 100 years. He is credited with many advancements, including building wooden houses, carts, and boats, as well as inventing writing.

- The turtle from the Lakota legend is an example of an earth diver. This term is used to describe a type of animal or being that is commonly found in flood and creation myths. In these stories, the earth diver plunges beneath the waves of a drowned world. It swims to the bottom and brings up mud. From the soil, new land and life is created.

- Llamas were an important part of the Incas' lives. Llamas carried people and supplies through the mountains. Their wool was used for clothes, and their dung made good fuel and fertilizer. People also used the animals' hides for leather and their meat for food. Tiny llama figurines were often buried with the dead, possibly as an offering to the gods.

- Many myths were told long before they were written down. The method of passing on stories, beliefs, and histories through speaking instead of writing is called an oral tradition.

GLOSSARY

cubit (KYOO-bit)—an ancient unit of measurement, which is equal to the distance from an adult male's elbow to the tip of his middle finger, or approximately 18 inches (46 centimeters)

culture (KUHL-chuhr)—a people's way of life, ideas, art, customs, and traditions

deluge (DEL-yooj)—a heavy rain; a great flood

dynasty (DYE-nuh-stee)—a series of rulers belonging to the same family or group

immortality (i-mor-TAL-i-tee)—the quality of being able to live forever

eternal (i-TUR-nuhl)—never ending

legend (LEJ-uhnd)—a story handed down from earlier times; legends are often based on fact, but cannot be proven to be completely true

mortality (mor-TAL-i-tee)—the quality of being able to die

myth (MITH)—a story told by people in ancient times; myths often tried to explain natural events

sacrifice (SAK-ruh-fise)—to offer something to a god or gods

tempest (TEM-pist)—a strong storm

READ MORE

Chambers, Catherine. *African Myths and Legends.* All About Myths. Chicago: Heinemann Raintree, 2013.

Ciovacco, Justine. *Discovering Native North American Cultures.* Exploring Ancient Civilizations. New York: Rosen Education Service, 2015.

Hoena, Blake. *Everything Mythology.* National Geographic Kids Everything. Washington, DC: National Geographic Children's Books, 2014.

Hynson, Colin. *Understanding Indian Myths.* New York: Crabtree Publishing Company, 2013.

CRITICAL THINKING QUESTIONS

1. Ancient peoples did not have the knowledge of the world we have today. So they used myths to explain natural events, from what caused floods to why the seasons changed. Myths were a way to understand the world. What other benefits might telling these stories have had for ancient peoples? What might people have learned from the myths in this book?

2. The Indian god Vishnu has three animal avatars — a fish, a turtle, and a boar. In the myth of Manu, how might the story have been different if Vishnu had come to Manu as one of his other animal avatars?

3. The flood myths in this book are hundreds to thousands of years old. They also come from many different parts of the world. Yet they share some similarities. Which myths in this book are most similar? What is the same and what is different? Are any similar to other stories you know?

INTERNET SITES

Use FactHound to find Internet sites related to this book.

Visit *www.facthound.com*

Just type in 9781515766278 and go!

 **Super-cool stuff!** Check out projects, games and lots more at **www.capstonekids.com**

INDEX